Wolverhampton

The way it was...

The buildings in Lichfield Street all dated from the last decade of the 19th century, so are barely 40 years old as trolleybus 43 (UK 4243), a Guy BTX with a 60-seat Dodson body that entered service on 20 November 1927, stands waiting at the junction of Lichfield Street and Princes Square. It is about 1936, as the Singer Bantam parked alongside the Criterion Hotel was introduced in that year and is therefore brand spanking new. The trolleybus is working on the 2 route to Whitmore Reans and has just left the town terminus in distant Victoria Square, where three six-wheel trolleybuses are parked, including one of the Sunbeam MS3s with a Birmingham-style body. Alongside the Singer is what appears to be a Morris Eight, but in truth could be a Standard Nine, a BSA 10hp saloon or something totally different! All are waiting at a predecessor of the

Belisha beacon crossing where girls from the High School are crossing the road. The distant trolleybus passing the Grand Theatre is one of the Guy-bodied Guy BTXs, of which one example, 78 (UK 9978), survives as a preserved hulk at the Black Country Living Museum in Dudley. Other identifiable motorcars include a big Ford V8 saloon and a Citroen 8CV. In the foreground on the right are the centrally mounted traffic lights around which the traffic appears to be moving without any apparent 'rule of the road'. Perhaps this accounts for the policeman standing outside the Criterion Hotel, who is adopting the pose of a disbelieving Edgar Kennedy, the Hollywood actor of the silent screen era known for his 'slow burn', who in comedy films often played the put-upon Irish-American cop. *J. Hughes collection*

Wolverhampton

A nostalgic tour by tram, trolleybus and bus

Part 3
The eastern routes

David Harvey
and
John Hughes

·ROAD TRANSPORT HERITAGE·
from
The NOSTALGIA Collection

First published in 2004

British Library Cataloguing in Publication Data

A catalogue record for this book is available from the British Library.

ISBN 1 85794 241 8

Silver Link Publishing Ltd
The Trundle
Ringstead Road
Great Addington
Kettering
Northants NN14 4BW

Tel/Fax: 01536 330588
email: sales@nostalgiacollection.com
Website: www.nostalgiacollection.com

Printed and bound in Great Britain

A Silver Link book
from
The NOSTALGIA Collection

Abbreviations

AEC	Associated Equipment Company	SOS	Shire's Own Specification
BCN	Birmingham Canal Navigations	UEC	United Electric Car Company
BET	British Electric Traction	WDET	Wolverhampton District Electric Tramways
BMMO	Birmingham & Midland Motor Omnibus Company	WMPTE	West Midlands Passenger Transport Executive
DS&WT	Dudley, Sedgley & Wolverhampton Tramways		
ER&TCW	Electric Railway & Tramway Carriage Works	**Seating capacity codes**	
FEDD	Front Entrance Double Decker	H30/26R	Highbridge, upper saloon capacity 30, lower saloon capacity 26, rear entrance
GWR	Great Western Railway		
LMS	London Midland & Scottish Railway	H-/-RO	As above, but open staircase
		H-/-F	As above, but front entrance
LNWR	London & North Western Railway	B38R	Single-decker bus, capacity 38, rear entrance
MCCW	Metropolitan-Cammell Carriage & Wagon Company		
		B-F	As above, but front entrance
MoWT	Ministry of War Transport	B-C	As above but centre entrance
PSV	Public Service Vehicle		

Contents

Only the tall radiator and the small headlights give away that 364 (DJW 364) is in fact a rebodied wartime vehicle. This Guy 'Arab' II originally had a MoS 'utility'-style Park Royal H30/26R body and entered service in 1943; its new elegant-looking body was supplied by Charles Roe in 1951. Of all the West Midlands municipal operators, only Coventry Corporation received bodies of this type, in its case on a selection of Daimler COA6s and CWA6s. No 364 is standing in Whitmore Street while 'lying over' before undertaking a further journey on the 40 route along Cannock Road as far as Brinsford. On the right is the Hickmans & Moulds dairy building, which would later become the Club Lafayette; this was *the* 'night-spot' to be seen at in 1970s Wolverhampton, and the building still exists today as the Rubicon Casino. Hickmans & Moulds, as well as producing and supplying milk, also made ice-cream, which was, by all accounts, truly revolting and had the consistency of putty! In the background, behind the three-wheeled Bond Minicar in the car park, is Bents public house, which would be swept away when the Ring Road was constructed. *A. D. Broughall*

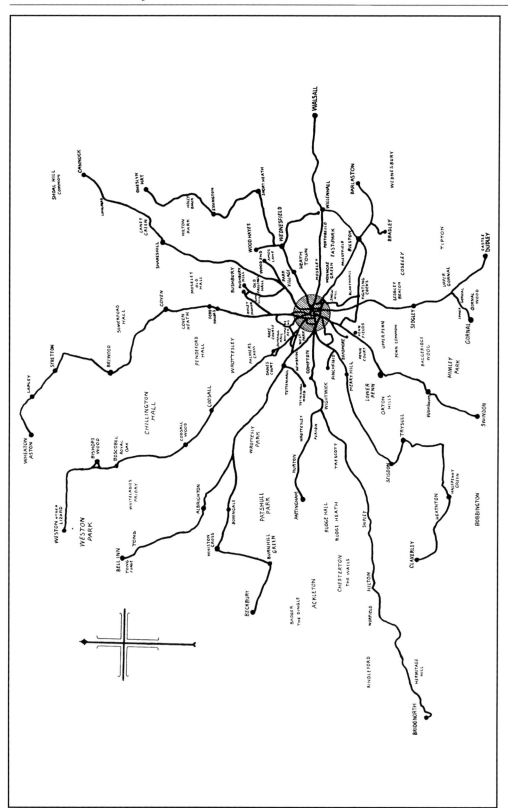

Routes operated by Wolverhampton Corporation Transport Department. The routes to the north-east and east are included in this book. These are the Cannock Road trolleybus services to Bushbury Hill, Pear Tree (Low Hill), and Amos Lane, the bus and trolleybus services along Wednesfield Road and beyond, Willenhall Road to Walsall, and to Bilston and Darlaston. Also included is the western half of the Darlaston route across the town to Whitmore Reans and the motor bus services beyond to Pendeford and Codsall.

Introduction

This is the third and final book to take a nostalgic tour of Wolverhampton by tram, trolleybus and bus, and basically takes in the remaining routes to the north-east around to the east of the town. The exception is the trolleybus route across the town to Whitmore Reans and the motor bus services beyond to Pendeford and Codsall. Included in Part 3 are the Cannock Road trolleybus services to Bushbury Hill, Pear Tree (Low Hill), and Amos Lane, together with the three arterial main-road bus and trolleybus services along Wednesfield Road and beyond, Willenhall Road and on to Walsall, and the other half of the Whitmore Reans service to Bilston and Darlaston. In addition, older photographs of tram operation are interspersed with the last of the Corporation's buses.

Many of the motor bus services are not as well covered as the tram and, especially, the trolleybus services, but this is simply because no one went to the places served by some of the more obscure bus routes, either in Wolverhampton's suburbs or out into the countryside. Suitable photographs are included where appropriate, but quite a few of these are in the town centre as, understandably, most bus photographers took their eight photographs just outside the bus station where they had just arrived!

A history of Wolverhampton Corporation serves as the Introductions to Parts 1 and 2.

Acknowledgements

Both authors have an extensive collection of Wolverhampton Corporation photographs that have been acquired over many years and these serve as the basis for this third Wolverhampton volume. Photographs from Alan Broughall, Clarence Carter, Alan Cross, Simon Dewey, Alistair Douglas, Jack Haddock, Robin Hannay, the late Bill Haynes, Malcolm Keeley, Jonathan Lewis of Eardley & Lewis of Wolverhampton, Roy Marshall, Les Mason, Robin Oliver, Douglas Parker, Paul Roberts, Mike Rooum, Colin Routh, W. Ryan, Tim Shuttleworth, Ray Simpson, R. Smith, Roger Taft, the late Stanley Webb, Ron Wellings, the late Ray Wilson and Deryk Vernon have all been a source of most useful photographs, as have all those photographers, including F. W. York, who supplied the late Bob Mack with negatives. Unfortunately, over the years the origins of many of the negatives have been lost. A number of early photographs have come from commercial postcards and from those wonderfully evocative plate photographs taken by Bennett Clarke of the life and times of everyday pre-war Wolverhampton, as well as those taken by O. Wildsmith on behalf of the Transport Department. Apologies are offered if we have missed anyone inadvertently from this long list. The late Cliff Brown's superb trolleybus photographs, all taken between 1958 and 1967, show Wolverhampton in a different age, before it was rebuilt with shopping centres and a ring road, when Stanley Cullis and Billy Wright ruled Molineux and long before it became a city.

We would like to thank Diana Harvey for her proof reading and to both Pam Hughes and Diana Harvey for putting up with countless meetings, their tea and sandwich-making skills, and patience and tolerance over many months.

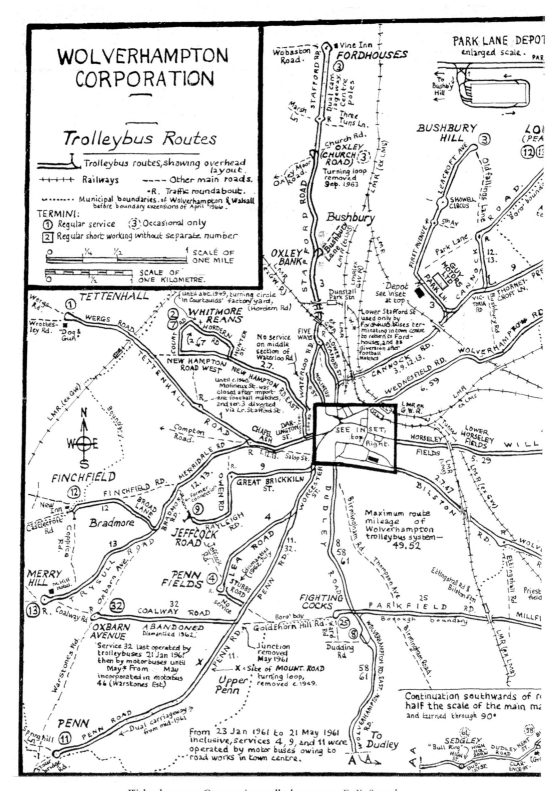

Wolverhampton Corporation trolleybus routes. *E. K. Stretch*

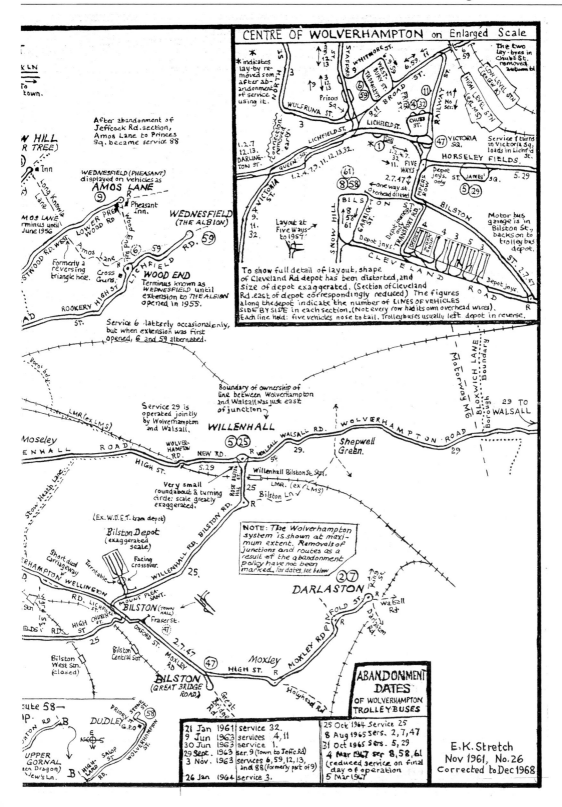

A special thanks must be made to Peter Townsend and his staff at Silver Link who had sufficient faith in this project to sanction what had been a one-book project into a definitive three-part work about Wolverhampton's road transport from the 1880s until 1 October 1969, when West Midlands PTE took over. Thanks are also due to Tony Lewis of The Black Eagle, Hockley, for his excellent CAMRA-approved ales, who allowed me to spend many long hours compiling this volume. Finally, there is our admiration for the patience and fortitude of the series editor, Will Adams, who crowbars mountains of irreplaceable photographs and reams of ever-expanding text into a book that makes the author's ideas a splendid reality!

A definitive bibliography is virtually impossible, but the PSV Circle publication *PD6* on West Midlands municipalities, and *2PD13* on the West Midlands PTE, have provided valuable vehicle information, while the highly recommended *A History of Wolverhampton Transport* Volumes 1 and 2 by Paul Addenbrooke, published by the BTHG, provides a well-researched factual account of the development of the Corporation's services. In addition, there are a wide variety of local history books that are too numerous to mention, but all contributed to the understanding of the changes in Wolverhampton from the 1880s to the present day, as do the Alan Godfrey reprinted Ordnance Survey maps, the originals dating from the Edwardian era, which proved so valuable.

David Harvey, Dudley
John Hughes, Wolverhampton

Despite Wolverhampton Corporation's pre-war allegiance to the Daimler COG5 chassis, only two wartime Daimlers were allocated to the Corporation. These were 382 and 383, which were the last wartime-specification buses to be delivered to the undertaking, arriving in early 1946. They were both Daimler CWD6s, ie with the newly introduced Daimler 8.6-litre CD6 engine, and both had Park Royal bodies built to the 'relaxed' utility pattern. Whereas identical buses delivered to nearby Birmingham City Transport were all withdrawn after about four years of service, the 'Wolverhampton Twins' managed some 15 years. It is perhaps surprising, in view of their preselector gearboxes, that they were not rebodied when all the Guy 'Arab' IIs were dealt with in 1950. No 382 (DUK 382) stands in Victoria Square when working on the 34 route to Blakeley Green. It is being overtaken by a six-cylinder 2215cc Wolseley 6/80 saloon, which was a favourite with police forces around the country in the late 1940s and early 1950s. Beyond the advertising hoardings is the imposing roof-line of the Prince Albert Hotel in Railway Street. *J. C. Brown*

Cannock Road routes

All the trolleybus services along Cannock Road, including those to Bushbury Hill, Pear Tree and Wood End, left the town centre by way of the gentle descent of Stafford Street, but on reaching the Elephant & Castle public house, all the routes turned right into Cannock Road. Here they plunged beneath three railway bridges, one of which was the former LNWR rail link that later became part of the electrified West Coast Main Line. These three bridges were so close together that they almost formed one continuous unit. As if this wasn't enough, the bus routes crossed a fourth bridge, which was the old GWR main line to Shrewsbury. From here until Park Village was reached, the area was a tight-knit community of Victorian terraced houses dominated by the Butler's Springfield Brewery and various foundries, including the Crown Galvanised Iron Works.

Immediately beyond the old Grand Junction Bushbury main line, the Bushbury Hill 3 trolleybus route turned left into Park Lane, passing Park Lane bus and trolleybus garage, which had opened on 25 July 1938. The north side of Park Lane was dominated by the huge Fallings Park Guy Motors factory and the engine manufacturer Henry Meadows. The Bushbury Hill trolleybus service was opened on 30 November 1931 and was coupled to the Stafford Road trolleybus service, which terminated at Fordhouses. The Bushbury Hill and Low Hill municipal housing estates were established in the mid-1920s and subsequent incursions by motor buses also began in the 1920s, with routes such as the 26 to Low Hill infilling the 'main-line' trolleybus service. At the trolleybus terminus was Old Fallings Lane, which was also the terminus of the 20 inter-urban motorbus route from Bushbury Hill to Willenhall via Wednesfield.

These huge interwar housing estates contrasted with the Cannock Road service, which continued through an ever newer series of housing zones. As well as the Cannock Road country bus services (see Part 2), the main transport provided by the Corporation was the 13 trolleybus, which, after passing through the suburban shopping centre at the Scotlands, descended a long hill to terminate at the County Borough boundary at the Pear Tree public house. The Cannock Road service was linked to Finchfield as the 12 service and to Merry Hill as 13 (see Part 2). The trolleybus service was opened on 21 March 1931, the same day as the third Cannock Road service, that to Amos Lane. This route was numbered 9 and was extended along Prestwood Road West to Wood End, linked across the town to Jeffcock Road (see Part 2). The route was lengthened to the Pheasant public house on 24 June 1956, becoming the last of Wolverhampton's trolleybus extensions.

All the Cannock Road trolleybus routes were abandoned on 3 November 1963 with the exception of the Bushbury Hill service, which survived for barely 12 weeks, finally going on 26 January 1964. The possible extension along Linthouse Lane through the early post-war housing estates never took place, but the extension to Wood End Road, by the motorbus 88 route, opened on 14 January 1951, while the Ashmore Park housing estate was served by the 68 motor bus route, introduced during 1963.

Stafford Street to Park Lane

Below Waiting for the traffic lights to change in Lichfield Street in about 1935 are three generations of pre-war Wolverhampton Corporation six-wheel trolleybuses. What is amazing is that the three double-deckers span barely seven years. Leading the queue at the junction with Princes Square is trolleybus 75 (UK 9975), a Guy BTX of 1931 vintage with a 59-seater body built by Guy itself. It is working on the 9B route to Low Hill (The Pear Tree) via Fallings Park, having worked into the town centre from either Finchfield or Merry Hill. Immediately following it is one of the 43-51 batch working into town on the 4 service from Penn Fields. It is a similar Guy BTX, but one of a batch built four years earlier,

at the end of 1927, whose Dodson bodies look positively archaic with their multi-windowed sides, rounded rear ends, albeit with totally enclosed staircases, and square, shed-like driver's cabs. The last trolleybus, working in from Mount Road, is a Sunbeam MS3 with a sleek-looking metal-framed Metro-Cammell body, which made even the 1931 Guy bodies look old! These were constructed to the same design as the Birmingham CT 17-66 class of Leyland TTBD2 trolleybuses. The front cab apron was deeper and had a larger expanse of yellow below the windscreen. Behind the bus is the Royal London Mutual Insurance Society building of 1902, while above the second trolleybus towers the Midland Bank, built in the Edwardian decade for the Metropolitan Bank. *D. R. Harvey collection*

Bottom The extension to the Wolverhampton & Staffordshire Technical College in Wulfruna Street, to the left of the recently reconstructed George Hotel, is well under way in this late-1932 view across Princes Square. Parked alongside the Vine Hotel in Stafford Street (right) is an unidentified Tilling-Stevens TS6 with a single-deck 36-seat Dodson body, which had been converted to pneumatic tyres about four years earlier. The single-decker is working on the 9 route from Amos Lane, only recently introduced on 21 March 1932. Turning in front of the George Hotel is Dodson-bodied double-deck Guy BTX trolleybus 60 (UK 6360). This is working on the 9B service to Low Hill Estate, which had also begun on 21 March 1932. The tall four-storey building next to the George is Wilcox's Rag Market, which would be replaced by further extensions to the Polytechnic. *J. Hughes collection*

The clock on the island at the entrance to Stafford Street shows 12.55 as the trolleybus moves around it, but the four attractive incandescent lamps above the four-sided clock are by this time out of use. No 415 (DUK 15), a Sunbeam W whose chassis dated from July 1945, turns back in Princes Square on a tight lock, and will hopefully just miss the 'PLEASE CROSS HERE' bollard on the Belisha beacon crossing at the entrance to Wulfruna Street. It is March 1962 and the 10-year-old replacement Park Royal body has emerged only a few days earlier from the Cleveland Road paintshops and positively gleams in the bright sunshine. Behind the trolleybus is the 'double-circled' Princes Square, with the Austin A40 emerging from Broad Street, while beyond that, passing Beverly's wine merchant, is an Austin A35 van, travelling towards the lower part of Lichfield Street with the round-fronted Mitchells & Butlers-owned Criterion Hotel occupying the corner site with Princes Street. The attractive, multi-coloured Baroque building, just in Lichfield Street, is the General Post Office. *J. C. Brown*

Below After the trolleybuses to Amos Lane were abandoned on 3 November 1963, the replacement bus route, numbered 68, was extended from the 1956 terminus at the Pheasant in Amos Lane into the Ashmore Park Estate in Wednesfield. The motorbuses took a much more direct route away from Princes Square, travelling straight down Broad Street, which prior to the First World War had been called Canal Street. The bus is 576 (KJW 576), a Guy 'Arab' IV with a Roe H31/25R body of September 1953 vintage, which somewhat ironically sat four fewer passengers than the trolleybuses that it had recently replaced on the Amos Lane route. The following bus is 140 (140 DDA), a Guy 'Arab' V with an 8.4-litre Gardner 6LW engine and a Park Royal H41/31F body. This larger vehicle, in its later all-over green livery, is working on the 59 service, which also terminated on Griffiths Drive, the circular link road serving the Ashmore Park housing estate. Effectively the 59 and 68 motorbus

routes were the circular extension of the 9 and 59 trolleybus routes along Linthouse Lane, proposed in the early 1950s but never implemented. *A. J. Douglas*

Bottom No 246 (AJW 46), a Sunbeam MS2 with a somewhat plainly styled Beadle H28/26R body, is parked in Stafford Street outside W. H. Wilcox's Rag Market, which pre-dates the Wolverhampton Polytechnic's National Foundry College next door, which was also demolished in the very early 1950s. The trolleybus is working on the 9 service to Amos Lane via Fallings Park in about 1948. Wadsworth's newsagent shop appears to have a good selection of national and local newspapers on sale, but unfortunately none of those on the outside rack gives any clue to the events of the day. No 246, although a Sunbeam, had been renovated by Guy, and the bodywork also extensively reconstructed, having overturned at Monmore Green in 1947; re-entering service on 15 November 1947, it was still withdrawn on 30 September 1949. Evident on the body, below the trolleybase supports, are the strengthening stays outside the second and third upper saloon body pillars. *R. Marshall*

Opposite page Looking towards Princes Square in Stafford Street on a busy Thursday, the people waiting at the Pear Tree trolleybus shelter must be casting an envious eye on the loading trolleybus standing at the 9 service stop. On 21 September 1961 No 405 (DJW 905) is on the Amos Lane via Fallings Park service, and is standing outside the 1950s Wolverhampton Polytechnic extension building. The trolleybus is a Sunbeam W4, which, with its original wartime 'utility' Park Royal body, had entered service on 30 November 1944. It was

rebodied in March 1952 with the somewhat plain-looking Park Royal body shown here. On the left is the wiring into Whitmore Street, which allowed the cross-town trolleybus 9 service to Jeffcock Road to lay over in the town centre. Beyond the Austin A35 van are two Roe-rebodied trolleybuses parked outside the Territorial Army's Drill Hall; the nearest is going to Fordhouses and is about to pull out and overtake 442 (EJW 442), which in turn will shortly leave for the cross-town journey to Finchfield. A Brush-bodied Guy 'Arab' III, which has passed the George Hotel as it turns from Wulfruna Street into Stafford Street, is working on the 33 route to Bushbury Church via Bushbury Lane. The terminus of this northern service was in Northwood Park Road, which was almost equidistant between the Fordhouses and Bushbury Hill trolleybus termini, whose 'in-and-out' service shared the same 3 route number.

Although 41 years have passed since the Corporation trolleybus 405 stood in roughly the same spot, the scene in Stafford Street has hardly altered. All the buildings from 1961 remain, though their ownership has changed, none more so than the Polytechnic, which is now the main campus for the University of Wolverhampton. Stafford Street has been widened in the intervening years, but with through-city car movements heavily restricted, most of the traffic is restricted to buses and goods delivery vehicles. The bus, 3007 (F307 XOF), a 73-seater MCW 'Metrobus' Mk II that entered service in December 1988, is standing in the bus lay-by on Monday 11 February 2002 and is loading up before going to Bushbury Hill on the 598 route. The pull-in lane is one of the few alterations to Stafford Street and was built after the days of the trolleybuses. *J. Hughes/D. R. Harvey*

Top Trolleybus 449 (EJW 449), a Sunbeam W4 rebodied by Roe in 1961, waits at the shelter in Stafford Street prior to leaving for Pear Tree, with the 1950s addition to the Wolverhampton Polytechnic building to its left. The long-gone wide pavement was 'decorated' with several large brick-enclosed flowerbeds, one of which is visible on the left. These somehow seemed to represent what every 1950s architect and town planner thought every town should have. Unfortunately, they were supposed to have flowers planted in them, but, with economic cuts taking place, they were often abandoned, leaving the bricked areas to become another receptacle for litter. Coming into town on the 3 route from Bushbury Hill is 405 (DJW 905), a wartime Sunbeam W4 with a 1952 Park Royal body. It is about to pass the junction with Whitmore Street, which was used from 1948 as the town terminus of the Jeffcock Road service, and carry on to stop beyond the Wolverhampton Registry Office outside the Drill Hall. Here the crews could get a quick cup of tea and perhaps a bacon or sausage 'sarnie' before whizzing off to the Fordhouses terminus in Stafford Road. Between the two trolleybuses is a two-tone Ford Anglia 105E, travelling towards the distant remnants of the row of Victorian premises in Charles Street, which shortly would be demolished to make way for the Ring Road. *C. W. Routh*

Middle Dennis Taylor's chemist shop, behind the kerb-side emergency fire telephone, both on the corner of Charles Street and Stafford Street, appears to be in the last throes of many years of service on 29 December 1963. It is selling Kodak film and has neat window displays of the sort that can still be seen today in the window of Emile Doo's chemist shop at the Black Country Living Museum – and remember that the museum's shop is supposed to represent one dating from about 1900! The buildings opposite have already been demolished prior to the construction of the Ring Road and the site has been railed off for use as a temporary car park with a controlled entrance. Coming out of Stafford Street on the 3 service to Bushbury Hill, with its saloon lights switched on, is Sunbeam W4 trolleybus 452 (EJW 452), which had entered service 15 years earlier with a Park Royal body, and returned rebodied by Roe on 14 September 1960. It was destined to be the penultimate service trolleybus from Dudley on the last day of Wolverhampton's trolleybus system. Towering above it is the five-storey block of the Wolverhampton Polytechnic. To the left is Faulkland Street, which for most of the last half of the 20th century contained the town's coach station. Behind the low wall was the site of St Mary's Church, closed in 1948 and subsequently demolished. *J. C. Brown*

Opposite bottom Coming into Stafford Street from Stafford Road towards the town centre is Sunbeam W4 trolleybus 449 (EJW 449), working on the 3 route and travelling to Fordhouses. This is the point where the present-day Ring Road cuts a great swathe across Stafford Street. As a result most of the buildings on the left, in distant Stafford Street, were demolished. On the right is the petrol station, garage and car showrooms of Charles Attwood; looking like a child's model, it dated from the 1930s and had embellishments more suited to an important council building than a garage. The showroom has for sale a couple of new Jaguar Mark IIs, a Triumph Herald and a Series II Land Rover. Following the trolleybus is a Volkswagen Kombi van, while parked outside Attwoods is a London-registered Austin A40 of 1960 vintage. *J. C. Brown*

Top right St Peter's Collegiate Church, in the town centre, was built at the highest part of the area, at some 529 feet above sea level, a commanding position that enabled it to be seen from all sides, and from Stafford Street its ghostly shape dominates the sky-line. The bright green and yellow-liveried trolleybus brightens up the dowdy, run-down urban landscape in Stafford Street as it descends from the town centre on 16 September 1963 towards the Elephant & Castle junction, where it will turn right into Cannock Road on the 12 route to Amos Lane. The trolleybus is 421 (DUK 821), one of the 1946 batch of Sunbeam W4 chassis rebodied by Charles Roe of Crossgates, Leeds. In this case the new H32/28R body was returned to service on 14 August 1958, but only had a working life of seven years in its new guise, being withdrawn when the Walsall route was closed on 31 October 1965. Parked outside Whitehouse's newsagent is a 1956-registered Ford Escort Estate 100E model, while behind it, in Nursery Street, is a 1489cc four-door Austin A55 Cambridge Countryman estate car, which had entered production at Longbridge in the spring of 1960. It is parked outside Hill's family grocery shop, one of the ubiquitous corner shops found throughout the inner areas of the town. Parked behind the trolleybus is a collection of 1950s British-built cars that would make a present-day enthusiast's mouth water, including a rather sumptuous R-Type Bentley. *J. C. Brown*

Above right Climbing Stafford Street away from the distant Banks's-owned Elephant & Castle public house on the corner with Cannock Road is one of the experimentally dark green-painted trolleybuses; Sunbeam W4 412 (DJW 942) was in this livery from December 1959 to March 1962. It is working into the town on its way to Jeffcock Road on the 9 route on 21 September 1961, and has just passed Wilson Street, which, like Herbert Street, off the picture to the right, was developed in the 1840s with a mixture of two- and three-storey housing; both side roads led into the former GWR Goods Station. This was also an area that contained a number of breweries, with the long-forgotten Russell's Brewery being located in Great Western Street and the Butler's Brewery in nearby Grimstone Street on the other side of the many railway lines. Fronting Stafford Road on the right is the wood merchant's yard of C. Walsh Graham, while behind the hoarding carrying advertisements for Ansell's Triple Gold, Smarties, Park Drive and, more anonymously, eggs, is the builder's yard of Braithwaite & Son. *J. C. Brown*

Below Turning right into Cannock Road from Stafford Street is, yet again, Roe-rebodied Sunbeam W4 trolleybus 421 (DUK 821). This attractively proportioned double-decker is, like the two railway footplatemen, passing the early-19th-century three-storey public house appropriately named The Junction. Opposite this old Ansell's hostelry, on the other side of Cannock Road, stood the later Victorian Banks's-owned Elephant & Castle – on the 1902 Ordnance Survey map, The Junction is shown as an Inn, while the other

was just a public house. By July 1962 most of the buildings around this junction were coming to the end of their lives and were demolished when the Stafford Street-Cannock Road-Lower Stafford Street was widened at the end of the 1960s as part of the Ring Road scheme. The overhead in the foreground allowed trolleybuses to travel in either direction along Lower Stafford Street, making a short-cut possible for those from the town centre to the junction of Waterloo Road and Stafford Road on the 3 route to Fordhouses. This was opened in the autumn of 1933 and was used mainly by trolleybus specials for the Wolverhampton Wanderers football matches at Molineux and the horse-racing at Dunstall Park. *J. C. Brown*

Below left Travelling along Cannock Road towards Park Village and about to disappear into the deep gloom of three railway overbridges is an Austin A125 Sheerline luxury saloon. The first two bridges were so close together that the overhead troughs were installed as one continuous unit, and they were followed by the old GWR's Victoria canal basin goods branch line. Climbing up the rise into town is the freshly repainted Sunbeam F4 trolleybus 474 (FJW 474). This Park Royal-bodied trolleybus had Wolverhampton's rather basic bodywork, which was prone to frame failure, necessitating a lot of maintenance expense; this resulted in the rapid deterioration of the bodies after the cessation of overhauls and the decimation of both the Guy BTs and the Sunbeam F4s. No 474 was withdrawn on 26 January 1964, only 28 months after its final overhaul and repaint. The former LNWR railway line, which today is part of the electrified West Coast Main Line, is carrying a mixed selection of enclosed goods wagons, though on the left is a consignment of BMW 'Isetta' 300s being delivered from the British factory at Brighton. *J. C. Brown*

Opposite right By the time the trolleybus routes to Bushbury Hill had been introduced on 30 November 1931, Cannock Road had been lowered sufficiently beneath the old LNWR railway line from Wolverhampton High Level station that it could be operated by double-deckers. The bridge had been re-opened on 16 August 1930 at the new lower level, the pedestrian walkway behind the railings on the left indicating the original road level. Shortly after the introduction of the 9A service, Guy BTX 68 (UK 8768), with a Dodson H30/31R six-bay body, passes through the damp darkness of the bridge. From the front these vehicles looked as though they were single-deckers with an added-on top deck, but they were among the first trolleybuses to have a one-step rear platform. No 68 entered service on 7 June 1930 and would remain so until, nominally at least, the last day of 1944. For many years subsequently it survived as a summer caravan at Borth, near Aberystwyth. *D. R. Harvey collection*

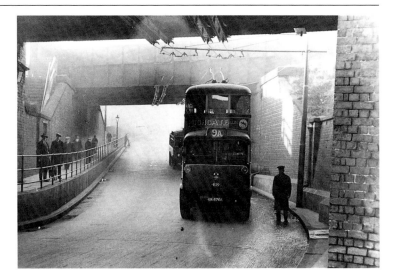

Middle On 15 September 1963, travelling on the 9 service to Amos Lane, is trolleybus 452 (EJW 452), a Sunbeam W4 that had been rebodied by Roe in 1960. As it passes over the former GWR line from Wolverhampton Low Level to Shrewsbury, it is being followed by an early Austin Seven, better known as a 'Mini'. To the left, behind the Esso garage sign, is Cambridge Street, home of Butler's Brewery; established by William Butler, by the 1950s it had become one of the largest in the Black Country, having 'hoovered up' a large number of other breweries throughout the West Midlands. It was taken over by Mitchells & Butlers in 1960 – the sign has not yet been altered –and still exists today. Just visible on the far side of the bridge in Cannock Road are the former premises of the Crown Galvanized Iron Works. *J. C. Brown*

Bottom Travelling out of Wolverhampton in Cannock Road is 446 (EJW 446), one of the 1948 batch of Roe-rebodied Sunbeam W4s, with its destination blind set incorrectly. On this miserable-looking Sunday, 29 December 1963, the trolleybus follows an Austin A40 Farina saloon towards Park Village; in the gloom on the extreme right is the parapet of the GWR underbridge seen in the previous photograph. They have just passed a row of extremely run-down Victorian terraced houses and a terrace of small shops, built on the site of Grimstone Farm, which had survived on the side of the Smestow Brook valley until the first decade of the 20th century. These houses and shops were themselves replaced in the late 1980s with an area of low-rise houses set well back from the road. In the foreground is a service road serving the 1960s Spring Valley maisonettes. *J. C. Brown*

This page The trolleybus powering its way up Cannock Road on its way from Bushbury Hill to Fordhouses is being overtaken by an Austin A30 two-door saloon, as they pass Prole Street and its Victorian terraces. On the left, outside the corner shop with its canvas canopy extended, the post-box has been freshly repainted. Working on the 3 route to Fordhouses on 3 November 1962 is 411 (DJW 941), one of the 1945 batch of Sunbeam W4s rebodied by Park Royal in 1952 with a body styling that had gone out of production some four years earlier. Behind the car is the start of a terrace of late-19th-century houses that extends down the hill into the distant Park Village.

The Optare XL single-decker, accelerating up the hill from the bus stop at Springfield Road, is Travel West Midlands 705 (S705 YOL), a 38-seater single-decker working on the 698 service into Wolverhampton on Saturday 23 February 2002. In the 40 years since the earlier view, the plane trees have grown, the post-box has disappeared and the house on the corner of Prole Street has gained a double-glazed porch. All the accoutrements of the trolleybuses have long since gone, but the shop remains, although it is perhaps a sign of the times that it now advertises Carlsberg lager rather than Twinings Tea. *W. Ryan/D. R. Harvey*

Above right On the corner of Woden Road and Cannock Road in Park Village, Murray's corner store was, in those far-away, pre-supermarket days, one of those little treasure troves that could nearly always be relied upon to have in stock whatever you wanted. In his side window, Mr Murray has put on a splendid array of soap powders and washing detergents, including such as Daz, Lux, Persil and Tide. Across the road was a Post Office, and almost hidden by the shop's canvas sunshade is a post-box with a stamp vending machine attached to it. This further railway bridge in Cannock Road, 15ft 6in high, is adorned with an advertisement for 'BUTLERS ALES', and carried what was Wolverhampton's first railway line into the town; this was the Grand Junction Railway's line from Manchester, opened for passengers on 4 July 1837, just two weeks after Queen Victoria succeeded to the throne. This pioneering main-line railway linked Wolverhampton, with its original nearby railway station at Heath Town, to Birmingham, and thence to London. By 3 November 1963 it had been part of BR's London Midland Region for 15 years, and would shortly be electrified as part of the West Coast Main Line scheme. Being so high, the railway bridge posed few problems for either the overhead wiring or the double-deck trolleybuses, such as 406 (DJW 906), with its Sunbeam W4 chassis dating from November 1944 and replacement Park Royal 54-seater body from March 1952. The level of traffic, even in this pre-'Swinging Sixties' period, is amazingly light, with only five identifiable vehicles, together with the 1957 Hillman Minx Series II travelling towards the distant Park Lane junction. *J. C. Brown*

Below right The overhead at the Cannock Road-Park Lane junction was a complicated set of span and support wires, tied to the traction poles that proliferated around the road. In bright sunlight, the shadows cast by the overhead wires on the road and the walls of the buildings look like a huge spider's web. On Monday 25 September 1961 8-foot-wide Sunbeam F4 466 (FJW 466) is working on the 9 route to Amos Lane. The driver wants to go straight across the junction in Cannock Road, whereupon the trolleybus will eventually cross the main road into Victoria Road a little bit further up the hill; the driver will be applying power to keep the overhead points from taking his booms into Park Lane. Following is an Austin A40, indicating that it is about to turn into Park Lane, and an Austin A55 van. Between the distant trolleybuses can be glimpsed the railway bridge seen in the previous photograph. On the extreme right is the wall of St Faith's Junior and Infant School, while behind the trolleybus is the Park Inn, which was, not unsurprisingly, supplied with its beers by the nearby Butler's Brewery. *J. C. Brown*

Park Lane to Bushbury Hill

Above After the closure of the Fordhouses 3 route and the Bushbury Hill 9 services on 26 January 1964, the trolleybus operation at Park Lane depot came to an end, and it became, for the first time, a bus garage. Once the last services had come in and those trolleybuses not being immediately withdrawn had been identified, the survivors were driven to Cleveland Road depot for further service, although a few did have a sojourn at Bilston depot, before it too closed in August 1965. Roe-rebodied Sunbeam W4 428 (DUK 428) is undertaking this manoeuvre as it turns out of Park Lane and into Cannock Road, followed by an almost new Park Royal-bodied Guy 'Arab' V. Behind the buses is St Faith's School, opened in 1893 by Heath Town UDC with places for 154

junior boys and girls and 189 infants; today it is the Park Village Community Centre. The signwriting on the gable end of the block of five late-1890s-built houses indicates the entrance to the Henry Meadows engine factory, some 200 yards away. On the left, a Morris 5cwt van, derived from the Morris Minor car, speeds through the Park Village junction towards the town centre. *J. C. Brown*

Below The rider of the Honda moped must be wondering what is going on as he approaches St Faith's School in Cannock Road on a cold night in early March 1964. The complicated overhead wiring at this junction was made redundant after the closure of the Fordhouses and Bushbury Hill trolleybus routes on 26 January 1964, and the same day also saw the closure of Park Lane depot as an operating base for trolleybuses. The abandonment of the 3 service saw off another 15 Guy BTs and six Sunbeam F4 8-foot-wide Park Royal trolleybuses. Despite the complexity of the wiring, amazingly the overhead here was pulled down within an hour, though some of it was saved for further use, as by 1962 there was only one national manufacturer of overhead material. The dismantling crew used two of the Corporation's tower wagons: manoeuvring in the middle of the road is WDA 301, the first of two 1959 Guy 'Warrior' tower wagons with bodies constructed in the town by a company called Robinson, while the other is one of the 1947 pair of Guy 'Vixen' tower wagons, EUK 770. *J. C. Brown*

Above right Turning into Park Lane from Cannock Road on Saturday 26 January 1963, with snow still lying on the ground, is Sunbeam F4 468 (FJW 468), one of only seven of this Park Royal-bodied 1948 batch to last into 1965. With its saloon windows steamed up, it is on its way to Bushbury Hill, so heavily laden with passengers that some are apparently standing on the staircase. A conductor, hitching a lift back to Park Lane depot, appears to be hanging on to the platform stanchion pole just as hard as he is holding in his left hand his waybill and cash box. Coming out of Park Lane is a locally registered 1960 Ford Consul II 204E four-door 'low-line' saloon; with a 1703cc engine, these were capable of 80mph and cost £773 when new. Behind the car and the trolleybus are the terraces built when Park Village was developed in the last years of the 19th century, including, just in front of the trolleybus, the end house in Wood Street, which has been converted into a corner shop. *W. Ryan*

Below On 18 January 1964 trolleybus 443 (EJW 443) emerges from the gloom near the Park Lane trolleybus depot. It is passing the huge Fallings Park factory of Guy Motors, as it swishes towards the Cannock Road junction. Sidney Guy set up his factory in 1914, having left Sunbeam earlier that year. By concentrating on small commercial vehicles and buses, Guy developed a reputation for sound engineering, though once it embarked on a 'big bus' policy, it rather lost its position in the 1930s bus market. Military orders became the 'bread and butter' of the company, but it was its spare capacity that helped to give it the contract to build the wartime 'Arab' bus. Names like 'Quad-Ant', 'Vixen', 'Otter', 'Warrior', 'Goliath' and 'Wulfrunian' all emerged from the Fallings Park works until financial disasters in the South African market resulted in the company going into receivership in October 1961 and being sold to Jaguar Cars Ltd in 1962. Despite having a full order book with its successful 'Big J' range of trucks, BLMC, by now the owners of Guy Motors, infamously closed the factory down in 1982, and within a few years most of the works was demolished and became a housing estate. *J. C. Brown*

Top The new six-road depot at Park Lane opened for trolleybus operation on Monday 25 July 1938 was situated opposite the Guy Motors works and next door to the Paget Arms public house, which dated from the late 1920s. This was at the north end of Park Lane overlooking where the Bushbury Hill trolleybuses turned into First Avenue. All the town's northern trolleybus routes were transferred to the new Park Lane site, and its opening allowed the antiquated Sedgley depot, with its forecourt turntable, to be closed on 31 October 1938. The lower front area of the building contained the traffic offices, while the engineering facilities were at the back of the garage – where else? Visible above the front service road are the trolleybus wires, which circuited the whole Park Lane site and were used to test new and recently repaired trolleybuses. The facility was also occasionally used by both Guy Motors and Sunbeam as a test track for their new trolleybus chassis intended for distant lands.

Once the trolleybuses had become established in their new depot, the north-side motorbus services were also operated from Park Lane *garage* after 30 April 1939 – remember that trolleybuses operate from *depots* and buses from *garages*! The official opening was delayed until Friday 6 October 1939, by which time the initial excitement of operating from new premises had become tempered by events elsewhere in Europe! Peeking out of the fourth bay is Guy BT trolleybus 262 (BDA 362), almost brand new, having entered service on 5 February 1938. It represented Wolverhampton's first contact with Leeds bodybuilder Charles Roe, which produced a very elegant-looking, compositely constructed body. Like all the pre-war trolleybuses, 262 was swept away in 1950 with the deliveries of the even less robustly Park Royal-bodied 8-foot-wide Guy BTs and Sunbeam F4s. *J. Hughes collection*

Middle and bottom Sunbeam W4 trolleybus 439 (EJW 439) turns out of Park Lane depot during the week between Christmas and New Year 1963, but minus its conductor, who is chasing after his charge; the driver is obviously unaware that his platform colleague is not aboard. Anyone who has ever been on a trolleybus will know that they have a phenomenal rate of acceleration up to about 20mph, so any chance of jumping on the platform of one that is just moving off is almost

certainly doomed to failure, unless you are an Olympic-standard sprinter. One wonders if one of the great 'Wulfrunians', Rome Olympics 100m bronze medallist Peter Radford, practised by chasing after his home town's trolleybuses? Behind is the perimeter service road that envelopes the whole depot site and was used for parking trolleybuses and buses. In this service road, beyond the Ford Anglia estate car, is a 'row of Roes', a line of rebodied early post-war Sunbeam W4 trolleybuses.

While the trolleybuses have long gone from Park Lane garage and there is now an imposing security fence around the premises, the steps from the traffic block on to the roof have surprisingly survived. On 2 March 2002 the fabric of garage looks in fine

fettle under the ownership of Travel West Midlands. It is now the only garage in the City of Wolverhampton and has an allocation of about 225 minibuses, midibuses, full-sized single-deckers and double-deckers, which compares to the 289 buses taken over from the former Wolverhampton Corporation fleet by West Midlands PTE on 1 October 1969. All the other garages have closed since the demise of the Corporation: the old Wolverhampton District garage in Mount Pleasant, Bilston, closed on 23 May 1971, Bilston Street combined with Cleveland Road garage on 13 September 1975, and the latter was finally vacated in the early 1990s after a period used to store redundant buses. *J. C. Brown/D. R. Harvey*

Top After Park Lane there followed an undulating though straight run of about a mile along First Avenue, spoiled only by the two traffic islands and the huge Showell Circus. The small three-storey block of early post-war shops, located between the triangle formed by First Avenue, on which the shops stood, and the other two sides of the triangle, rather confusingly both named Guy Avenue, were in sight of the Paget Arms public house. On the last day of trolleybus

operation on the Bushbury Hill service, 26 January 1964, Sunbeam W4 452 (EJW 452), which had only re-entered service with its smart new Roe 60-seater body in September 1960, passes the shops on its way into town. In the intervening years little has changed at this location, save for the installation of a traffic island that occupies the large space in the foreground. *J. C. Brown*

Above The other end of the Low Hill route 26 is seen in the mid-1960s. This route started in the town at School Street and went in a westerly direction from Chapel Ash by way of Whitmore Reans, Gorsebrook Road and into Bushbury Lane, turning into Hammond Avenue before terminating at Kempthorne Avenue. No 5 (SUK 5), a Metro-Cammell-bodied Guy 'Arab' IV of March 1957, and one of 12 of that year's dozen and a half that were fitted with a Meadows 6DC engine, has just come down Darlington Street, in the background, and is negotiating the Ring Road island at Chapel Ash. This was the second phase of the Ring Road to be opened, between Penn Road and Chapel Ash, and is seen soon after completion, judging by the somewhat sterile-looking buildings. *D. R. Harvey collection*

Above On a miserable winter's day another of the Roe-rebodied Sunbeam W4 trolleybuses, 444 (EJW 444), has travelled up the hill from Park Lane and is negotiating the island in First Avenue at the Fifth Avenue junction on its way towards Showell Circus and the Bushbury terminus. To the right of 444, destined to be the last Finchfield trolleybus, is the entrance to Goodyear Avenue, a reminder of the proximity of the Goodyear Tyre factory, whose first brick was laid in 1927, only about a year after the Low Hill and Bushbury Hill housing estates had been begun. *J. C. Brown*

Below Showell Circus was the centre of the large housing estate at Low Hill. Here, as well as the original row of 11 shops, with their deeply gabled roofs and dormer second-floor windows,

was that other essential of suburban life, the pub! The Bushbury Arms, a typically large, mock 'Tudo-Eliza-Jaco-Art Deco' piece of suburban public house architecture, was opened in 1929 and was originally owned by Atkinson's Brewery. Just visible on the right is Low Hill Library, opened in 1930 with a hexagonal main reading room surmounted by a large central lantern. Parked outside the Bushbury Arms is Guy BTX trolleybus 61 (UK 6361), a Dodson-bodied Guy BTX trolleybus that entered service on 15 May 1929 and belonged to the first generation of large trolleybuses that had long gone beyond the 'trackless tram' stage, yet had entered something of a cul-de-sac of evolution that would only be resolved when the 'big' bus builders decided to adapt motorbus chassis for trolleybus operation. Thus Guy Motors, Ransomes, Simms & Jefferies and Karrier all produced similar-looking six-wheeled leviathans at the end of the 'Swinging Twenties'. The Wolverhampton trolleys, all built by Guy, had a typically high-mounted body, in this case built by Dodson, with a very globular enclosed rear end and a top cover that was, at least from the side, modern-looking, although it was somewhat 'perched' above a very tram-styled lower saloon. *D. R. Harvey collection*

Above right The original part of the Low Hill Estate, with Showell Circus shopping area at its heart, comprised some 600 houses, but was soon extended to cover nearly 500 acres of the former estate land of Low Hill House, built in 1760 for Willis Kempson of Bilston. Latterly owned by the Lovatt family, who owned the internationally respected civil

engineering and construction company, the large Georgian house, with its lovely large Victorian conservatory, went into a rapid decline after the Great War and was demolished in 1926. On Boxing Day 1963, just one month before the conversion to motorbus operation, trolleybus 442 (EJW 442), a Sunbeam W4 rebodied by Roe, re-entering service on 1 August 1960, goes around the eastern side of Showell Circus on its way into Wolverhampton. It is passing the junction with Annan Avenue and is about to overtake the Surrey-registered, eight-month-old Series II Land Rover parked outside the main group of shops. Behind the trolleybus, on the corner of Leacroft Avenue, is Low Hill Methodist church; it foundation stone was laid on 29 September 1928, and it was consecrated in 1929. *J. C. Brown*

Below The 'Garden City' movement, which had its origins with Quaker industrialists such as Thomas Lever at Port Sunlight and the Cadburys at Bournville, and was developed by Ebenezer Howard at Letchworth and Welwyn Garden City, had an enormous effect on post-First World War urban planning throughout the country, including Wolverhampton. David Lloyd George's promise to make 'Britain a fit country for heroes to live in' might have been a little over-optimistic, but the resulting wide roads, grass verges, tree-lined avenues and a garden for everyone was certainly a better proposition than the slums of inner Wolverhampton. Climbing into his cab at the Low Hills terminus is the driver of bus 31 (DA 9031), a 1924-built Tilling-Stevens TS6 with a Dodson body, while his conductor stands in the rear entrance of the 36-seater. This service had been introduced on 5 December 1927, and within a year motorbus services were instituted to Merry Hill and Fighting Cocks at the junction of Hammond Avenue, formerly named Twelfth Avenue and Leacroft Avenue. *Commercial postcard*

Above The wide open spaces of 1920s and '30s housing estates, such as that at Low Hill, somehow seemed to suit the silent trolleybus as a mode of transport. As the householder in the front garden on the right tends to his plants while wearing the almost obligatory cap, braces, Fair Isle sleeveless pullover and rolled-up shirt sleeves, a pair of 'silent servants' trundle along Leacroft Avenue. Several trolleybus operators actually trained their drivers on passenger-carrying services, but Wolverhampton did not adopt this policy and a trainee driver would go out in a vehicle slotted between normal service trolleybuses. No 423 (DUK 823) is passing the entrance to Hillcrest Avenue and carries an L-plate in the nearside windscreen. Following this Roe-rebodied Sunbeam W4 is 8-foot-wide Sunbeam F4 464 (FJW 464), whose driver has already changed the destination blind for his next journey to Fordhouses. *C. Carter*

Below The Wolverhampton Corporation Act of 1926 enabled the local authority to extend the Borough boundaries, and new housing estates were built to replace the town's inner area slums. On 16 July 1928 the recently introduced motorbus service was extended from Low Hill to Bushbury Hill, where the terminus of the 9A route was at the junction of Leacroft Avenue and Old Fallings Lane, and was converted to trolleybus operation on 30 November 1931. Guy BTX trolleybus 57 (UK 6357), fitted with a totally enclosed Dodson H33/28R body embellished with a somewhat prosaic advertisement for BOVRIL, was the first of a class of five delivered in the first days of May 1929. It is at the recently established Bushbury Hill terminus, a matter of days after the trolleybuses had been introduced, judging by the still new-looking Council-owned housing in Leacroft Avenue and the still fairly sparse-looking trees and shrubs. *D. R. Harvey collection*

Above right The road junction at the Bushbury Hill terminus enabled the trolleybuses to have a large turning circle. This must have been entertaining for day-dreaming schoolboys in the nearby Bushbury Hill Junior and Infant School, who, in the classrooms overlooking the turning circle, could watch a succession of trolleybuses unloading, turning and re-loading at the terminus. Standing at the terminus and about to descend Leacroft Avenue on the 3 route in December 1963 is Sunbeam W4 435 (EJW 435); its chassis dated from April 1947 and was rebodied by Charles Roe, returning to service on 1 January 1962. While the 3 route would be closed on 26 January 1964, 435 would survive until the last day of the system on 5 March 1967. On the left is the Unloading Only stop for the trolleybuses arriving at the turning circle

at Old Fallings Lane, while another trolleybus of the same type negotiates the turning circle. To the right, behind the neatly trimmed privet hedge, is a row of the typical Council-built houses dating from the late 1920s, which were at the northern margin of the Low Hill overspill area, while on the left is a Wolverhampton-registered Phase VII Hillman Minx. *W. A. Camwell*

Right Old Fallings Lane, Bushbury Hill, was also the western terminus of the inter-urban motorbus 20 route. The open spaces that led to Bushbury Hill and the lovely old Georgian Bushbury Hall lie behind the double-decker, which is parked directly opposite the terminus of the Bushbury Hill trolleybuses at Leacroft Avenue, and while the trolleybuses did their 180-degree turn, coming from the south, the 20 service did the same, though obviously without the overhead wiring, from the east. The 20

bus route started on 15 February 1926, when the Corporation took over the service from an operator called Ray who ran from Wood End Road via Wednesfield to Willenhall. It meandered its way from Bushbury Hill, crossing Cannock Road at The Scotlands shops, before eventually turning south-eastwards and crossing the Amos Lane trolleybus service at the Red Lion public house. The 20 route then went through Wednesfield before completing its semi-circular course in Willenhall, this latter part, after the

1949 route renumbering, having its own number of 50 for this intensely used shortworking. The bus is 571 (KJW 571), a Guy 'Arab' IV with a Gardner 6LW and a Roe H31/25R body, which entered service in September 1953. It belonged to a batch of seven buses that, in the West Midlands at least, were unique in that they were Roe bodies on new chassis as opposed to rebodied wartime buses and trolleybuses. It survived to be taken over by the WMPTE but was taken out of service in 1971. *R. Taft*

Low Hill (Pear Tree)

Below The trolleybuses working beyond Park Lane along Cannock Road all turned off the main road into Victoria Road. Trolleybus 426 (DUK 826) stops at the Victoria Road junction on 16 September 1963 in order to allow a Commer Walk-Thru 1½-ton van to pass along Cannock Road. Behind the trolleybus is the Fallings Park Garden Suburb, an attempt by Sir Richard Paget, the local landowner, to produce Wolverhampton's answer to Port Sunlight and Bournville. He devoted 400 acres of land around the Old Fallings Hall estate to the proposed Garden Suburb and the first house in this ambitious scheme was opened by the Bishop of Lichfield on 26 February 1908. By the outbreak of the First World War only about 100 houses had been built, the municipally built and owned houses of the 1920s post-war 'brave new world' having succeeded the philanthropic and idealistic efforts of late-Victorian industrialists. In the distance, on the skyline, is the junction to the left with Bushbury Road, from where the trolleybus started at Pear Tree on its journey into the town centre and on to Merry Hill. It is a 1946 Sunbeam W4, the first of the 38 rebodied trolleybuses to be returned from the Charles Roe works, re-entering service on 6 August 1958. *J. C. Brown*

Above right The trolleybus turning right into Victoria Road from Bushbury Road on Sunday 15 September 1963 is on the 12 route from the Pear Tree terminus on Cannock Road, working across the town centre to Finchfield. Both the 12 service from Finchfield and the 13 service from Merry Hill strangely retained their separate numbers when travelling to and from their northern terminus at Pear Tree. The shops,

almost hiding beneath the trees on the right, are on the corner of Thornycroft Lane and Bushbury Road, and were passed by the Amos Lane 9 trolleybus route. To the left of the trolleybus is an emergency 999 telephone; these were usually for police use, but some were painted red and members of the public could use them to summon the fire brigade, if of course they knew the location of the nearest box. One is reminded of Robb Wilton's famous fireman's sketch in which he said to the woman on the other end of the telephone, 'Well, can you keep it going until we get there?' The trolleybus is 447 (EJW 447), a Sunbeam W4 that entered service with its original Park Royal body on 23 December 1947, and re-entered service with this Roe body on 18 April 1961, lasting until the last day of trolleybus operation on 5 March 1967. *J. C. Brown*

Below right The trolleybuses regained Cannock Road after running along the two sides of the triangle via Victoria Road and Bushbury Road. Cannock Road is in the background, at the 1930s Golden Lion public house, and the Ford Cortina Mk I four-door saloon is turning to take the 'straight-line' route into Wolverhampton, which is the route that motorbuses took. The trolleybus is 455 (EJW 455), numerically the last of the Roe-rebodied Sunbeam W4s originally built in 1948. It is coming into town along Bushbury Road on 15 September 1963 working on the 13 route to Merry Hill. On the right is the impressive four-doored fire station, while behind the trolleybus is a Mobil petrol station. Through the tall poplar trees are the 1950s Princess Court maisonettes in Kingsway, while just visible is the tower of Our Lady of Perpetual Succour Roman Catholic church opposite Old Fallings Lane, Bushbury. *J. C. Brown*

This page Going out of town along Cannock Road is Roe-rebodied Sunbeam W4 trolleybus 422 (DUK 822), negotiating the neatly maintained traffic island, with Old Fallings Lane on the right behind the railings. At this roundabout the main A460 took the right turn going out of town, so the trolleybus is coming from the left, from Cannock Road's town side. In front of the trolleybus is the site of the future Old Fallings United Reform Church. On the far side of the island is Park Lane, which until the end of the First World War was part of the old Bushbury Parish boundary and was a pretty little country lane; subsequently lined with 1920s municipal housing, in 1963 it leads to a junction opposite the Paget Arms public house next to Park Lane bus garage. The shadow on the left is cast by Roman Catholic church of Our Lady of Perpetual Succour, while the shadow of the railings marks St Mary's RC Junior and Infant School. The church's foundation stone was laid on 13 September 1933 and it was opened on 29 June 1934, but someone forgot to consecrate it! This was only discovered when the church was celebrating its 50th anniversary, so it was finally consecrated on 19 October 1999. Therefore, are all those Catholic marriages in the intervening 55 years strictly legal…?

On Saturday 2 March 2002 one of Choice Travel's pair of rare Wright-bodied Mercedes-Benz OH 1416s negotiates the same island on its way to Underhill. The Wednesbury-based independent's bus, 32 (N32 EVT), which entered service in October 1995, is operating on the 511 service; they were sold in 2003. Since 1963 the large mature trees around the traffic island have been replaced and much of the vegetation has been cut down, so while a car driver's view around the obstacle is much better, it does look less attractive. On the right, in front of the Old Fallings United Reform Church, are railings to prevent pedestrians from running out into the road, while the old-fashioned KEEP LEFT signs have been replaced by white arrows on a blue background. *J. C. Brown/D. R. Harvey*

Opposite top On Sunday 15 September 1963, a bright sunny autumn day, two proud parents push their young baby in the sparkling new pram along Cannock Road. Parked on the other side of the main road, almost at the Croft Lane junction, is one of the original Ford Escorts; these were little more than a Ford Thames 300E van with windows. This one dates from November 1956 and was registered in nearby Staffordshire. This section of Cannock Road was lined with late inter-war semi-detached houses, and swishing along beneath the trolley wires, working on the 12 route, is Sunbeam W4 trolleybus 403 (DJW 903), having left the Deyncourt Road bus shelter on its way in to Wolverhampton. Originally fitted with a Park Royal utility body and entering service on 5 December 1944, after eight years these wartime bodies were becoming badly worn, so 403 and 15 similar vehicles were rebodied, again by the London-based bodybuilder, 403 re-entering service on 1 March 1952. *J. C. Brown*

Middle Standing at the Mill Lane bus stop on Cannock Road is a pre-war trolleybus that has come from the Pear Tree terminus about half a mile away, on its way across the town to Merry Hill on the 13 route. Behind the trolleybus, on the right, is a row of single-storey shops that continued to the traffic island at Primrose Lane, while to the left the land has yet to be built upon and is still rough ground covered by trees and grass. At this time, the late 1940s, the trolleybus overhead along this section of the route was hung beneath bracket arms. The trolleybus is 281 (BJW 181), a Guy BT with a rather elegant-looking Roe H29/25R body, which entered service on 17 September 1938. Guy's BT model was not a very common type, with only 39 being built between 1934 and 1939, 27 of which were bought by the local operator. No 281 was the last pre-war Guy trolleybus to be purchased by Wolverhampton Corporation. *S. N. J. White*

Bottom Passing that row of unusual single-storey shops in Cannock Road is Guy BT 634 (FJW 634), a Park Royal-bodied 54-seater trolleybus that entered service on 1 December 1949. By 5 October 1963 the 'old girl' has less than four months of service left in front of her before withdrawal when the Bushbury Hill and Fordhouses services are abandoned. Note that the trolleybus overhead is by now suspended from span wires, rather than the more expensive bracket arms. The wiring itself is remarkably taut and in good condition, despite the route to Pear Tree being condemned to closure in less than a month on 3 November. The shops were constructed around the Primrose Lane junction, which led to the pre-war 'Scotlands' housing estate, where many of the roads were named after famous English poets and novelists. The shops include Mills's general store, Simmonds's wallpaper and paint store, and an ironmonger and a chemist. Parked beyond the shops is a Standard Vanguard III, a Wolseley 15/50, a Standard Eight and a Hillman Minx Series III, while on the left, facing the town centre, is a 1960-registered Austin Mini Seven. *J. C. Brown*

Above Climbing up the hill from the Pear Tree terminus towards the Primrose Lane island is trolleybus 449 (EJW 449), a Roe-rebodied Sunbeam W4 working on the 13 service across the town to Merry Hill on 15 September 1963. Following the trolleybus is a Standard Eight Tourer of 1947. To the left of the wide open grassy space, which, although threatened with becoming part of a dual carriageway in Cannock Road, still remains to the present day, are the 1950s houses that form part of the Underhill Estate. The houses on the east side of Cannock Road were in Wednesfield UDC, which was absorbed by Wolverhampton in 1966. On the extreme right, just before the rows of 1920s houses begin, is the yard of Happy Times Coaches of Wednesfield, whose noticeboard advertises that it has 14- to 36-seaters for hire. The double-decker bus is GKT 549, a former Maidstone & District 'unfrozen' Bristol K5G, with a chassis dating from 1942 and fitted with a new 1952 Weymann body. It was

bought in October 1961 and lasted until May 1965, but it couldn't have done much work as it was photographed in July 1962 in exactly the same position! *J. C. Brown*

Below Coming down the hill in the opposite direction is 404 (DJW 904), one of the old-fashioned-looking Park Royal-rebodied Sunbeam W4s. Hills like this were 'bread and butter' for trolleybuses, which could effortlessly power their way up the hills and silently glide and swish their way down the other side. In 'swishing mode' 403 is on the 13 service near the Low Hill terminus on 19 May 1963. The bus stop in the foreground is the unloading point for the terminus, with the sign reading 'BEWARE BUSES TURNING'. On the Wednesfield (left) side of Cannock Road are privately owned villas and bungalows built in the 1920s. *W. Ryan*

Opposite top The 1950s housing at the edge of the Underhill Estate spilled over on to Cannock Road, which formed the boundary between Wolverhampton and Wednesfield UDC. The Cannock Road terminus of the 12 and 13 trolleybus routes at Low Hill took its name after the Pear Tree public house, and was contrived by simply widening the out-of-town, Wolverhampton side of the road. This is still here today, although the Pear Tree pub has been renamed The Mill House and the junction with Pear Tree Lane in the foreground is now controlled by traffic lights. The rather splendid overhead turning circle really shows that this was 'the end of the line'. On 5 October 1963 the driver of 473 (FJW 473), a 95hp BTH-powered Sunbeam F4, on the 12 route, waits until the Triumph Herald has

sped past on its way into the town centre before hauling his charge around to the terminus pick-up point opposite the Pear Tree Inn. Waiting in the lay-by is Roe-rebodied Sunbeam W4 423 (DUK 823), working on the 12 route to Finchfield, which is being overtaken by a West Bromwich-registered Austin 5-ton normal-control lorry dating from 1956. *J. C. Brown*

Middle With the Pear Tree public house in the background, Bournemouth Corporation trolleybus 129 (BEL 814), one of its splendid two-door 1935 Park Royal-bodied Sunbeam MS2s, waits at the Cannock Road terminus stop before embarking on the return cross-town 12A service to Finchfield. This was the County Borough boundary, so Pear Tree Lane was the end of the line as far as the trolleybus route was concerned. Bournemouth's 129 arrived in Wolverhampton on 28 October 1940 and was only returned to the seaside resort on 7 December 1948, having just been fully overhauled and repainted in Cleveland Road depot. Apparently it looked immaculate! It was the last of the 12 Bournemouth MS2s to remain in Wolverhampton. *F. W. Shuttleworth*

Bottom Of the 464 Sunbeam W4 trolleybuses built between February 1943, when the model was introduced, and September 1948, when the last of the type entered service in Johannesburg, South Africa, no fewer than 155 received wartime Park Royal 'utility-style' bodies. No 430 (DUK 830) was a late chassis, numbered 50308, which entered service on 5 June 1946 and had the 137th wartime Park Royal trolleybus body to be constructed. By this time the concession to peace-time standards meant that 430 had upholstered seating and extra opening side saloon windows, but still retained the squared-up wartime body outline. It is seen in Cannock Road parked just beyond the Pear Tree Inn, facing Wolverhampton, working on the 12 service to Finchfield in about 1952, not long after it had received its second repaint, on 4 January 1952. It was taken out of service in April 1959 and was sent to Charles Roe of Crossgates, Leeds, re-entering service with a new 60-seater body on 7 September of the same year. It is adorned with an advertisement for the wonderful Elkes Biscuits – do you remember their custard creams? *R. V. Taft*

Amos Lane

This page From Victoria Road, with the Bushbury Road junction to the right and Fallings Park in the background, the Amos Lane 9 service carried straight on into Thorneycroft Lane. Roe-rebodied Sunbeam W4 trolleybus 421 (DUK 821) is doing precisely that manoeuvre on 23 September 1961 as it works outwards to the Lower Prestwood Road terminus about 1½ miles away. In the distance, travelling towards the town centre, is an FJW-registered Park Royal-bodied trolleybus, passing the Fallings Park Garden Suburb of 1908. This area was in Heath Town, which was a civil parish formed in 1866 and became an Urban District Council in 1894. In the latter part of the 19th century a certain amount of ribbon development along the roads radiating out to the north of Wolverhampton took place. Clusters of house were also developed around road junctions, with houses such as those on the left in Bushbury Road. Parked under the trees on the right, in front of a curve of small shops, are two Hillman Minx Series IIIs, dating from about 1960. The traction pole on the left carries electrical power supply cables feeding into the overhead, while on the right there is a third, unconnected, piece of powered trolleybus wire; this went from Bushbury Road around the corner into Thorneycroft Lane, but strangely was apparently never used.

Crossing the same junction from Victoria Road on 2 March 2002 is Optare Excel 700 (S170 YOL), a 38-seater single-decker and one of 35 that entered service between January and March 1999 from Wolverhampton's Park Lane garage. It is following a 1991 Rover 800 as it enters Thorneycroft Lane, working on the 527 service to Ashmore Park operated by Travel West Midlands. The shops on the right are largely closed, though the Bass-owned Bird in Hand public house, dating from the mid-19th century, which the bus is approaching, seems to be a thriving hostelry. The traffic at the junction is controlled these days by traffic lights, while pedestrians have to negotiate a maze of protective steel railings in order to cross the road. Behind the bus are some of the Fallings Park Garden Suburb houses, with their faintly 'Arts and Crafts' gabled roofs. *J. C. Brown/ D. R. Harvey*

Above Both the in-bound and out-bound trolleybus overhead wiring in Prestwood Road West was suspended from single bracket arms, with the traction poles being planted on the eastern side of the road. On 20 September 1961 quite recently re-varnished Roe-rebodied Sunbeam W4 423 (DUK 823), destined to be the last Jeffcock Road trolleybus, travels up the slight gradient towards the Prestwood public house and the nearby 1930s telephone exchange. Coincidentally, the trolleybus is working on the 9 route to the aforementioned Jeffcock Road. The tree-lined Prestwood Road West was a product of the 1920s, as shown by the detached house on the right, although around the Prestwood Road junction there are a small cluster of late-Victorian houses. Parked on the left is a Glamorgan County Council-registered Bedford CA Mark I van of June 1954. *J. C. Brown*

Above right The original Amos Lane route, with a terminus at the Red Lion public house, was brought into use on Monday 21 March 1932, on the same day as the Pear Tree service opened. By that time the standard Wolverhampton trolleybus was a six-wheeled Guy BTX, but within four years the Corporation's policy had changed and all new vehicles after the delivery of trolleybus 245 were four-wheelers. The standard post-war trolleybus was an 8-foot-wide vehicle bodied by Park Royal and mounted on either a Guy BT or Sunbeam F4 chassis, both of which were manufactured in Wolverhampton. At the Red Lion, the trolleybuses had to reverse, using a reverser, into Amos Lane

in order to turn around to face Prestwood Road West, before travelling back to the town. Here 462 (FJW 462), a Sunbeam F4 of September 1948, reverses into Amos Lane; the Red Lion, with its mock-Tudor mullioned windows, is on the right. This manoeuvre was photographed just prior to the extension of the trolleybus route; careful examination of the picture shows a roped tie-off on the left, suggesting that the wiring for the reverser had already been prepared for abandonment. This happened on 24 June 1956, and the last new extension on Wolverhampton's trolleybus system was opened at the same time, taking the trolleybuses straight across the Amos Lane junction to follow Lower Prestwood Road for just over one-third of a mile to the Pheasant public house at Wood End Road. *D. Vernon*

Below Looking across Amos Lane from the forecourt of the Red Lion public house, we see the very 1930s-looking shops on the corner of Prestwood Road West. Contrasting with the 1930s semi-detached houses in Prestwood Road West, the shops, with their almost flat roofs and square windows, were by 23 September 1961 occupied by Mitchell's grocery shop, Bennett's confectionery outlet, Denton's fruit and vegetable store and Simcox, the butchers. The forecourt was used both by potential customers and the shopkeepers, and on this autumn Saturday an Austin A40 Devon Countryman and a much later Bedford CAL Martin Walker caravan conversion are parked outside the shops. Crossing Amos Lane at the original terminus into Lower Prestwood Road is Sunbeam W4 trolleybus 421 (DUK 821), which by this time had been working with its replacement Roe body for just over three years. Following the trolleybus is one of Wolverhampton Steam Laundry's Austin 30cwt delivery vans. *J. C. Brown*

Below left The wide open space on the west side of Lower Prestwood Road always looked as though it should be made into a dual carriageway, but has survived until the present day. Roe-rebodied Sunbeam W4 trolleybus 426 (DUK 826) unloads its passengers while the driver anxiously looks through the bulkhead windows to see if his conductor is ready to 'ring him off'. This early 1960s view obviously pre-dates the 'Swinging Sixties', as there is only evidence of the Ra-Ra skirt, with its flared hems, among the women getting off the trolleybus and the girls on the other side of the road. The trolleybus has only a short way to go to the terminus and looks virtually empty, so the driver's keenness to get away is probably so that he can enjoy a quick cigarette before returning to the town centre and on to Jeffcock Road. *A. A. Turner*

Opposite top Returning to town along Lower Prestwood Road on 20 September 1961 is 414 (DUK 14), one of the wartime Sunbeam W4 trolleybuses rebodied in 1952 by Park Royal. This vehicle lasted until the closure of the north-east routes in the town, which included Pear Tree, this service to Wood End, Wednesfield and their cross-town connections to Finchfield and Merry Hill. This occurred on 3 November 1963, and not only decimated these early rebodied trolleybuses but also the town's trolleybus system, sounding the 'death knell' for the survival of the system. But that is another two years away as 414, followed by an Austin A35 Countryman, glides away from the terminus; in the foreground is the service road for the 1950s municipal housing estate, lying unused. *J. C. Brown*

Opposite middle About 2½ miles away to the north-east was the Mossley terminus of the Walsall Corporation trolleybus system, which was also on the boundary with Staffordshire. The extension had been opened on 3 June 1957 and marked an 'Indian summer'

of new trolleybus routes in that town. The Amos Lane extension in Wolverhampton to the same Staffordshire boundary at the Pheasant public house at Wood End Road was opened on 24 June 1956 to serve the same sort of 1950s housing development, and might have been seen as the beginning of a similar series of trolleybus route extensions in the town; what is forgotten is that Wednesfield UDC had requested this extension to the Pheasant public house as long ago as April 1939. Unfortunately, in June 1957 Wolverhampton Transport Committee, despite the need to conserve fuel oil after the recent Suez Canal crisis, decided that the trolleybus system had reached its maximum size. This led to the decision in May 1961 to gradually wind down the trolleybuses in the town as and when vehicles and infrastructure became ready for replacement. So the Pheasant extension was Wolverhampton's trolleybus 'swan song', despite the similarities found in nearby Walsall. Roe-rebodied Sunbeam W4 trolleybus 437 (EJW 437) negotiates the island at the Pheasant public house island at Wood End Road, with its row of early 1950s shops in the background. Behind the trolleybus is the Staffordshire boundary and the open countryside beyond towards the nearby village of Essington. *W. A. Camwell*

Bottom With the large Pheasant public house in the background, trolleybus 416 (DUK 16), another of the 1952 Park Royal-rebodied wartime Sunbeam W4s, waits at the Wood End terminus stop before embarking on the return cross-town 9 service to Jeffcock Road via Great Brickkiln Street. As if to remind the trolleybus driver that he has to follow the overhead wires back into the town, the Council has kindly provided one of the same sort of road signs that Dinky Toys made as a model in the 1950s, indicating that there is a traffic island, or, as we used to call them, 'a roundabout', ahead. The circle of shops at Wood End Road's junction with Lower Prestwood Road at the County Boundary served as an excellent terminal point for the trolleybuses, being the northern focus for the housing and its local population. Yet this need not have been the case as there was a proposal to extend the service to Wednesfield Road at the Albion to make a circular service with the 59 trolleybus route. Alas, it never happened. *J. C. Brown*

Fighting Cocks, Bilston and Willenhall

The 25 trolleybus service began on 27 October 1930 and was Wolverhampton's only interurban trolleybus route. Its history, however, was that it was actually a truncated version of the Wolverhampton District overhead tramcar service that was opened in stages from Dudley, finally reaching Fighting Cocks on 9 January 1902. On 14 July 1902, Company operation was extended from Fighting Cocks to Bilston, but after much bickering, overhead and Lorain dual-equipped trams were enabled to run directly between Dudley and the Corporation's Snow Hill terminus in Wolverhampton after 15 October 1906. The route was extended from the existing Fighting Cocks to Bilston and Darlaston on 1 May 1907, then came the reversion to Dudley, Fighting Cocks & Darlaston Company operation on 11 January 1909 after Wolverhampton Corporation refused to erect overhead wires from Snow Hill to Fighting Cocks, the Wolverhampton District Company having complained that the added weight of the Lorain equipment was becoming expensive. It was only after the 8 service was converted to overhead wiring through to Dudley on 26 March 1921 that Company operation resumed on the Wolverhampton to Fighting Cocks route. This was finally abandoned in November 1926, but the Fighting Cocks to Bilston and Willenhall route remained in Company operation until it was taken over briefly by Wolverhampton Corporation on 1 September 1928. The Fighting Cocks to Bilston section was closed on 25 November 1928 and the short branch to Bradley went just five days later.

On 27 October 1930 the Corporation's equivalent of the former Company tram service was introduced between Fighting Cocks, Bilston and Willenhall, only this time it was the 25 trolleybus route. At Willenhall Market Place it turned round back into Bilston Street crossing the Walsall 29 trolleybus route. Operationally it was only altered twice, first on 8 October 1934 when a new turning circle was put in at Dudding Road about 200 yards along the 58 route in Wolverhampton Road (shades of the Company trams to Dudley), and on 8 May 1949, when the Fighting Cocks terminus was moved once again along Goldthorn Hill as far as the first road on the left, Ward Road, where a large turning circle was installed. The 25 route's premature closure was effected on 27 October 1964 because of the necessity to rebuild Waterglade railway bridge at Willenhall station over the West Coast Main Line. The route was operated by 12 hired-in former Birmingham CT Daimler CVD6s, despite the opportunity to put in a temporary turning circle just short of the offending railway bridge at Rose Hill Gardens.

The route from Goldthorn Hill ran across the end of the Birmingham New Road and the 97 Thompson Avenue bus service, and within yards of the terminus of the 30 motorbus service to Rough Hills. Continuing through industrial Ettingshall, the 25 route reached Bilston's shopping centre. Until the replacement motorbuses came in 1964, it was the only public service route to traverse High Street, Bilston, passing the historic half-timbered Greyhound public house, which dated from the 1450s. The trolleybus route crossed over the old Great Western Railway line at Bilston's Central railway station, which today is part of the Midland Metro. After turning hard left at Bilston's now derelict Town Hall into Lichfield Street, with its attractive Regency buildings, the route climbed towards Wolverhampton before turning right into Mount Pleasant where the Bilston trolleybus depot and its turntable was located.

The remainder of the route, along wide sweeping suburban roads lined with mainly inter-war housing, such as Willenhall Road and Bilston Road, were ideally suited to fast, silent trolleybus running. A sharp left turn saw the trolleybuses into Rose Hill, which led them to the terminus at Willenhall.

Above When the 25 trolleybus service was first opened on 27 October 1930, its Fighting Cocks terminus was in Wolverhampton Road East at Dudding Road, which it shared with the in-bound trolleybus services from Dudley; this was within yards of the original Wolverhampton District tramcar terminus. On 8 May 1949, in order to relieve congestion at this turning loop, the 25 service was given a new turning circle at Ward Road. In the summer of that year Sunbeam W4 trolleybus 431 (DUK 831), still with its original 'semi-utility' Park Royal body, stands at the new terminus beneath the extensive overhead wiring that formed the turn-back loop. In the background, where the distant lorry is leaving Dudley Road, is the famous Fighting Cocks junction. The properties on Goldthorn Hill's north side, on the left, were generally of late-Victorian origin, though the house on the extreme left dates from the 1920s. The properties on the right behind the trolleybus are part of the inter-war Goldthorn Park housing development. Had the 25 trolleybus been extended beyond this point it would have crested Goldthorn Hill and descended to meet the trolleybus services in Penn Road, and opposite the 32 Coalway Road service. But it was not to be! *J. Hughes collection*

Right In December 1959 six trolleybuses were repainted in an experimental green livery. One of the former utility-bodied Sunbeam W4s, 412 (DJW 942), rebodied by Park Royal in March 1952, begins its long journey to Willenhall on the 25 service from the Ward Road turning circle. In the background the houses climb towards the crest of Goldthorn Hill, with those on the left generally dating from around the beginning of the 20th century. The trolleybuses had to make a tight turn out of the terminus; in this case the progress of 412 is not helped by the parked Ford 300E van. *J. C. Brown*

Top　On the right, alongside the Fighting Cocks public house, leaving Wolverhampton Road East and about to turn into Parkfield Road, is Wolverhampton District open-top bogie car 23, built by Brush in 1902 and en route to Bilston using the overhead system. On the left, standing at its terminus in Dudley Road, is a Corporation tram working on the Lorain stud system. The photograph was taken between 8 March 1904, when the Corporation trams were extended to Fighting Cocks, and 15 October 1906, when the company cars were fitted with the heavy Lorain skates in order to work directly into Dudley. *J. Hughes collection*

Middle　The building on the corner of Dudley Road and Parkfield Road, behind the traffic lights, is the one outside which the Corporation tramcar was standing in the previous photograph. Trolleybus 625 (FJW 625), a 95hp Sunbeam F4 with a Park Royal H28/26R body that entered service on 29 March 1950, crosses the Dudley trolleybus wires at Fighting Cocks and begins to power its way up Goldthorn Hill towards the Ward Road terminus of the 25 service in about 1952. It is being followed by a Morris Oxford MO and a Morris Eight, while travelling into Parkfield Road is a Bedford Utilicon van dating from about 1947. *C. Carter*

Bottom　While the trilby-hatted gentleman pedals into Goldthorn Hill, trolleybus 486 (FJW 486), a Guy BT that entered service in July 1949, follows the 1956 Sheffield-registered Volkswagen 'Beetle' 1200 across the Fighting Cocks junction working on the 25 service on 15 April 1963. This Park Royal-bodied vehicle is fitted with a white steering wheel, signifying that it is 8 feet wide. The trolleybus overhead that crosses almost at right-angles serves the Sedgley and Dudley trolleybuses. Following the Guy is a two-door Morris Minor that is about to turn into Dudley Road in front of the row of shops. These dated from the 1920s, and although their frontages were dominated by what looked like structural concrete pillars, behind the facades they were just standard brick-built premises. Dominating the corner site, behind the 'parked' Silver Cross perambulator, is the largest shop in the block; this was owned by D. A. Rimmer, whose phone number is the fairly unforgettable 57000. *J. C. Brown*

Right The original terminus of the 25 trolleybus route was in Wolverhampton Road East at the Dudding Road turning circle, and the route shared the loop with the Fighting Cocks 8 service, the first of the Dudley trolleybus shortworkings. On 13 April 1946 trolleybus 202 (JW 3402), a Guy BTX with a Metro-Cammell H33/25R body that entered service on 10 February 1934, stands in front of the inter-war semi-detached houses that formed the eastern edge of the Goldthorn Park Estate. Alongside 202 are a pair of pre-war Park Royal-bodied Sunbeam MF2 four-wheeled trolleybuses, working on the 8 route into the Snow Hill terminus in Wolverhampton town centre. No 202 still displays the remnants of its white wartime blackout paintwork, which

suggests that the vehicle was in dire need of a repaint, having had its last paint and varnish in May 1943. It was one of five Guy BTXs that had Birmingham-style straight-staircase bodies, which were very similar to the 17-66 class of Leyland TTBD2s supplied to convert the Coventry Road trams to trolleybus operation on 7 January 1934. *R. Hannay*

Below The stretch of Parkfield Road between Fighting Cocks and the intersection at Birmingham New Road was built up with a succession of Victorian terraces, interspersed with open land. The space on the right had been part of Cockshutts Colliery, which functioned well into the 20th century and was well known for its Carboniferous Club

Moss fossils. Much later, in 1961, Guy BT 487 (FJW 487) approaches the Parkfield Tavern and the overhead feeder point, over which it will have to coast in order not to blow the circuit-breakers in the cab, rendering the trolleybus immobile. The old-style orange road sign on the left displays information for the A41 to Newport, the A449 to Kidderminster, the A454 to Bridgnorth and the A459 to Sedgley and Dudley. Following the trolleybus is a be-bumpered tractor, which has obviously escaped from its factory duties, while an Austin A35 and a pre-war Austin Cambridge travel towards Fighting Cocks. Today the vacant site on the right is occupied by the Parkfield Health Centre. *J. C. Brown*

Below The Atkinson Silver Knight eight-wheeler lorry turning into Birmingham New Road is fitted with a Gardner 6LW engine and, for its time, a pioneering moulded glass-fibre cab. The Roe-rebodied Sunbeam W4 trolleybus, 431 (DUK 831), is travelling along Parkfield Road on the 25 service towards Bilston on 17 March 1961. This trolleybus received its new 60-seat body on 18 November 1958 and would remain in service until 11 July 1966. Waiting at the traffic lights on the right is a Dodge Kew 5-ton tipper lorry, while turning into Thompson Avenue is an April 1955-registered Hillman Minx Phase VI. The municipal houses in Thompson Avenue stand on the reclaimed Cockshutts Colliery and were built in the early 1920s. *J. C. Brown*

Bottom Once past the busy Birmingham New Road junction (A4123), Parkfield Road continued eastwards to Ettingshall. Speeding towards the former LNWR railway bridge is an Austin A35 van, while pulling away from the bus stop outside the little 'huckster' shop is 8-foot-wide trolleybus 480 (FJW 480), the penultimate member of the 1948 batch of Park Royal-bodied Sunbeam F4s. It has passed Myatt Avenue, just behind the parked Standard Pennant, on 24 June 1961 on its way to Bilston and Willenhall on the 25 route, and still looks smart, having been repainted only six months previously in December 1960. On this lovely sunny, summer Saturday, a young girl pushes her young sibling in her mum's new two-tone pram past the row of Victorian houses that had been built opposite the old Parkfield brickworks. *J. C. Brown*

Above right Immediately before reaching Ettingshall Road, Parkfield Road swept beneath the bridge carrying the former LNWR Stour Valley railway line. The bridge also

carried the platforms of Ettingshall Road & Bilston station, opened on the 1 July 1852 when the LNWR opened its line and seven intermediate stations between Birmingham New Street and Wolverhampton. The station closed on 15 June 1964 having become redundant after the closure of many of the ironworks in the area, though the railway line exists as part of the much-criticised electrified main line between Birmingham and Wolverhampton. Trolleybus 484 (FJW 484), a Guy BT with a Park Royal H28/26R body, comes under the bridge on 17 March 1961 as it approaches Ettingshall Road junction and the Union Mill public house, another long-since-closed hostelry, which occupied a small triangle of land between the corner of

Manor Road and the railway embankment. Following the trolleybus is a Rover 12 of July 1939 and an early 1950s Humber Imperial, which has seen better days and is being used as a taxi. *J. C. Brown*

Below Dominating Millfields Road, between Ettingshall Road and Millfields Bridge over the Wolverhampton Level of the Birmingham Canal, was the Ettingshall Boiler Works of John L. Thompson, built in 1870 to make large industrial boilers, tubes and general heavy engineering materials. A feature of the Thompson works was its reliance on traction engines to move heavy materials by road, as many of the manufactured products were too large for any of the railway company's loading gauges. Eight-foot-wide Guy BT

trolleybus 488 (FJW 488), working towards Bilston on 15 March 1961, passes Thompson's gaunt brick and corrugated steel buildings, having left behind the old Britannia Boiler Tube works on the corner of the distant Ettingshall Road. This tall wall separates the steel-workers from the rest of the world – indeed, these large Black Country heavy engineering centres were a world of their own. On the extreme right are the 'seven daughters' houses, which were reputedly built by a local industrialist for each of his girls, and officially known as Millfield Terrace. The traction pole on the pavement outside carries electricity feeder cables for the trolleybus overhead. Yet among this industry, planted in the front gardens of the houses, must have been the loneliest trees in Ettingshall. *J. C. Brown*

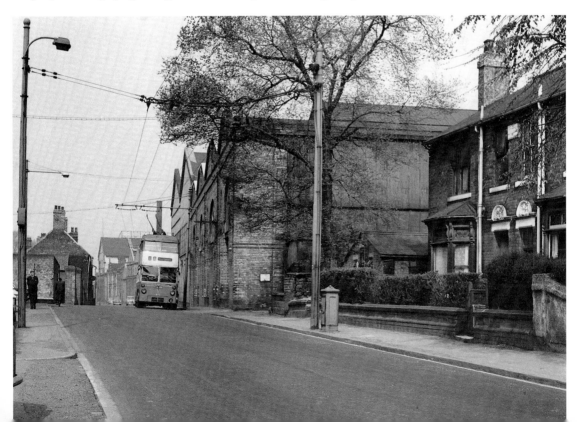

Below Yet another 8-foot-wide Park Royal-bodied Guy BT, 489 (FJW 489), working on the 25 service, crests the BCN's Millfields Road canal bridge on its way towards Bilston and Willenhall. One of the strange features of the Black Country's urban geography was the juxtaposition of land uses. Here is a good example, with the end block of a terrace of inter-war houses next door to the old factory premises of Thomas Bantock, who repaired both canal narrow-boats and GWR railway wagons. Mr Bantock later bought Merridale House, which was quickly renamed Bantock

House in Bradmore Road. The son, Albert Baldwin Bantock, who was later thrice Wolverhampton's mayor, refurbished the interior of the house in the 'Arts and Crafts' style, which always appeared to have a 'touch' of the bargees' art in it. In the background are the industrial buildings of the Bilston Gas Works. One of the problems of operating trolleybuses was their inability to overtake easily, so the driver will just have to wait behind the little Bedford 30cwt pick-up and the tractor with its home-made jib and sloping cradle. *J. C. Brown*

Bottom   Before reaching Bilston, Millfields Road crossed the 'Old Worse and Worse' railway line, its unaffectionate nickname derived from the appalling record of the Oxford, Worcester & Wolverhampton Railway, latterly part of the Great Western Railway. The 'top of the town' in Bilston was where Coseley Road, to the right, met Wolverhampton Street, to the left, and where Millfields Road became High Street. On 9 November 1961 Guy BT 496 (FJW 496), with its destination blind incorrectly set, emerges from the deep shadows of High Street and begins to accelerate across the busy junction. Although the black and white steel railings encouraged pedestrians not to walk across the junction, it was not protected by traffic lights. Behind the trolleybus, outside the Bird in Hand public house, is a Ford Anglia 105E.

Ironically, opposite this pub was the Primitive Methodist Church, occupying the corner site at Thompson Street, which would be closed during the following 12 months. The three-storey block dominating the junction has already seen better days, and in fact the middle shop is empty. To the left of the trolleybus is a sweet shop and confectioner, while the end shop, owned by G. Bowden, who incidentally appears to be peeking from behind the upstairs net curtains, sells children's schoolwear. The Noah's Ark was an early-19th-century building that was by now a de-licensed public house masquerading in its death throes as a travel agency. *J. C. Brown*

Right At the western end of High Street is the wonderful half-timbered Greyhound and Punchbowl public house. It was built in about 1450 as Stowheath Manor House and originally with eight gables. Just beyond this architectural treasure is the corner of Hartsthorn Street. On the other side of the road, just visible on the left, is the little Mitchells & Butler's-owned Golden Cup public house. The 1930s block beyond the pub was mainly occupied by Sammy Dale's furniture shop, though Young's butcher shop occupied the unit next to the pub. To the right of the approaching trolleybus is the Plough Inn and The Swan pub, which was a Banks's house. On Saturday 15 April 1961 trolleybus 480 (FJW 480), a Sunbeam F4, drifts almost silently down High Street as it travels towards Bilston town centre. It is about to overtake a Morris Y 10cwt van, whose semi-forward control layout was unusual, though it had been copied by the more successful Fordson E83A. With its 1,547cc side-valve engine and three-speed gearbox, the Morris Y, originally introduced in 1939, resumed for another four years its post-war production in 1946. Parked outside Hartill's electrical shop is a one-year-old Staffordshire-registered Austin A99 Westminster. Staffordshire was the first local licensing authority to issue reverse registrations, as long ago as 22 April

1953. On the right, with its fish and chip shop next door waiting to catch the trade of late-night film-goers, is the Savoy Cinema, which was within a few years of closing. *J. C. Brown*

Above right Passing the impressive frontage of Dale Forty's furniture shop in High Street as it approaches Pinfold Street is 412 (DJW 942), one of the six experimentally dark green-painted trolleybuses. A Sunbeam W4 chassis, it entered service on 5 May 1945 with a Park Royal utility body, re-entering service with a 54-seat Park Royal body on 18 March

1952. It is travelling towards Bilston Town Hall on 15 April 1961, passing many of the buildings dating from the mid-Victorian period, including the Leopard public house and John Stern's tailor shop, established in 1865 when Dudley House was new. To the left of the Triumph Herald Convertible is the Bilston branch of Marks & Spencer; when it closed, this 1930s-vintage building became part of a much-enlarged Kwik Save supermarket. Next door is Peters ladies' dress shop, a wet fish shop and, beyond the alley, the Ansell's-owned Balloon Inn. *J. C. Brown*

Top Two trolleybuses have just passed each other in Church Street, Bilston, on 28 March 1961. The one approaching is 497 (FJW 497), a Guy BT built in September 1949 with a 95hp BTH motor and an 8-foot-wide Park Royal body, working on the 25 service towards Fighting Cocks. The row of single-storey shops on the right stands on an extra width of bridging built in the 1950s over the impressively deep cutting through which ran the former GWR main line between Birmingham Snow Hill and Wolverhampton Low Level. When the Midland Metro station was built in the 1990s, these buildings had been demolished so that access could be gained to the Birmingham-side platforms. Hidden by the pedestrians on the left is St Leonard's graveyard, while the classically styled church, dating from 1826, was 'round the corner' in Walsall Street. In front of the receding Dudley-registered Morris Cowley 1500 is another Wolverhampton Corporation trolleybus working to Willenhall, though route numbers were not displayed on the rear destination blind. Towering over the trolleybus is the imposing Bilston Town Hall, which stands at the awkward junction with the distant Lichfield Street. *J. C. Brown*

Middle Tram 16, one of the 56-seater Ansaldo T69s built in Italy in 1998, picks up passengers at Bilston Central on the Midland Metro Line 1 on 16 August 1999, as it works between St Georges, Wolverhampton, and Birmingham Snow Hill Station. The Metro platforms are in the old deep blue-brick railway cutting and are staggered on a curve because of the confined width. The platforms next to the new Bilston bus station are the main entrance, being reached by stairs and a lift on the Wolverhampton platform. The distant steps serving the Birmingham-bound platform descend from Church Street, located exactly where Broadmead's radio and television shop was in the previous photograph. Bilston's original GWR station was slightly out of the town to the south-east, but after the end of passenger services between Birmingham and Wolverhampton in March 1972, the planning and construction of the A463 Black Country Route cut through the original station site, rendering its re-instatement impossible. The opening of the architecturally adventurous bus station between the Black Country Route, the new open-air market site and Church Street in the 1980s led to this cutting in Bilston town centre being utilised as the new station site, allowing the bus station to be transformed into that terrible name, 'the interchange'! The first day of operation was Monday 31 May 1999. *D. R. Harvey*

Opposite bottom Bilston was first served by trolleybuses on 19 November 1928 when the Corporation route to Bilston from the town centre replacing the 7 tram route, and this in turn was extended to Darlaston, some six months later on 28 May 1929. Therefore the Fighting Cocks-Bilston-Willenhall 25 trolleybus route, which followed the old Wolverhampton District company service, was the second trolleybus route to reach Bilston on 27 October 1930, and went straight through to Willenhall, passing the Bilston depot in Mount Pleasant on the way. The trolleybus, again the dark green-painted 412 (DJW 942), a 1952-rebodied wartime Sunbeam W4, stops at the Belisha crossing while a Wolseley 4/44 and a Hillman Minx queue behind it. It is about to undertake the left turn in front of Bilston Town Hall from Church Street into Lichfield Street, and is following an Austin A55 car. This was a manoeuvre that would have been impossible in tram days as there was no track that went directly in front of the Town Hall; any tramcar coming from Church Street wanting to get to Bilston depot would have to turn into Lichfield Street, then reverse across two sets of points in order to regain the Wolverhampton-bound tracks going towards Mount Pleasant. *J. C. Brown*

Above right A Ford Consul II 206E is caught in a traffic jam in Lichfield Street, at the busy junction where a set of trolleybus wires takes the 25 route into Mount Pleasant. It is following what appears to be a complete production facility of the then Milk Marketing Board: a battery-electric milk float and a lorry carrying milk churns. Having turned out of Mount Pleasant, Guy BT trolleybus 492 (FJW 492) travels past Clark's Café and the Odeon Cinema

towards Bilston Town Hall. The cinema had opened on Thursday 17 November 1921 as Wood's Palace, with a seating capacity of 1,400. The café, opened at the same time, was originally called the Palace Café. The trees on the left were in front of the delightful Regency Parsonage, while on the corner of Wellington Road the three-storey brick building with the porticoed entrance is Wellington House. *J. C. Brown*

Above Another Park Royal-bodied Guy BT, 489 (FJW 489), turns into Lichfield Street from Mount Pleasant on the 25

service, which will take it through Bilston and on towards Fighting Cocks. The second trolleybus is 482 (FJW 482), which has just left Bilston trolleybus depot and will shortly take up duties on the cross-town 2 service to Whitmore Reans. The car waiting to turn right between them is an Austin A40 Devon, while behind 482 is a Ford Consul EOTA, then one of its big sisters, a Ford Zodiac Mk I EOTA. Parked outside the long-since-demolished Globe Hotel and opposite the old Theatre Royal is a Burlingham 'Seagull'-bodied coach. *J. C. Brown*

Above On 19 June 1962 Guy BT trolleybus 605 (FJW 605) turns into Bilston trolleybus depot, having completed its tour of duty on the 25 route. Company operation of tramcars was taken over by the Corporation on 1 September 1928 when the Willenhall to Darlaston via Bilston services commenced. The Corporation took over 15 tramcars, which included seven single-deckers, three small four-wheeled 50-seater double-deckers, and five large bogie cars. In addition, some 61 staff, including 18 drivers and 18 conductors, were taken on, while Bilston tram depot was also included in the deal. This took place just five days after the final closure of the indigenous Corporation tram services, the 7 route to Bilston. The Grade II listed depot, opened in 1900, closed when the final 'final' tramway abandonment of the inherited tramways was completed on 30 November 1928, then re-opened for trolleybus operation on 27 October 1930, being converted to motor bus operation from 26 October 1964. Depot House, at 34 Mount Pleasant, with the letters 'WDET' carved into its frieze, is also a Grade II listed building; originally the home of the Wolverhampton District tramway company manager, in later Corporation days Howard Davies, the Chief Traffic Motor inspector for many years, lived there. Because of the small yard, trolleybuses had to be turned on a turntable, making this the second depot on the system to have one, the other being in Sedgley (there were only two others in the country, at Huddersfield, and at Christchurch on the Bournemouth system). Parked on the pavement in front of the depot is a black Austin A30, a Standard Ten and a Ford Anglia 105E with its reverse-angled rear saloon window. On the left is a Fighting Cocks-bound trolleybus, parked outside a row of very run-down cottages, the last one being used as a tobacconist where many a driver bought his 'fags' for the lay-overs during his day's duty. Behind the trolleybus is one of Pathfinder Coaches' Duple-bodied Bedfords, while behind 605 can be made out the gap between the Midland Electric Power Company building and the distant shops,

occupied by the Theatre Royal of 1901 before it was demolished in 1961. *J. C. Brown*

Above right On a sunny day in June 1961 two workmen pedal passed the Albion Works of Bradley & Co, which had rebuilt its factory in the 1950s. If you were a housewife in the early post-war years, you stood a good chance of owning one of Bradley's products, such as buckets, bowls and baths – its best-selling product, under the brand name of Beldray, was an ironing-board! The trolleybus, 491 (FJW 491), is travelling out of Bilston town centre along a section of Mount Pleasant lined with late-Victorian houses partly hidden by tall trees. Its driver has just switched on the trafficator and looks into his mirror before pulling away from the trolleybus stop. *J. C. Brown*

Right Trolleybus 475 (FJW 475) has travelled from Bunker's Hill Lane and is working its way towards Willenhall on the 25 route on 13 April 1961. The unusually titled Bunker's Hill Lane was named after the battle of Bunker's Hill, the first battle of the American War of Independence in 1775. This Bilston end of Willenhall Road really marked the end of the Victorian residential developments to the north-east of Bilston, and on the left can be seen a few inter-war local authority houses. The vehicle is a Sunbeam F4 with a Park Royal H28/26R body, which entered service on 16 October 1948. Despite having a final repaint in January 1963, it was withdrawn just one year later when the Fordhouses and Bushbury Hill service was converted to motorbus operation. It is passing the present Cock Inn nearly opposite Lonsdale Road, which has a Standard Vanguard Phase I, with a couple of oddly painted front wings, parked on the forecourt. The original Cock Inn was in a small 'green' off Willenhall Road, while its replacement was designed to serve the new 1930s housing estate. The few remaining Victorian houses that used to be around the old open space are to the right of the pub sign. *J. C. Brown*

Above Further along Willenhall Road, the junction with Moseley Road marked the boundary between Bilston and Darlaston, and the change from predominantly council housing to late inter-war semi-detached houses. Having sped past these houses on 4 June 1962, the trolleybus, Guy BT 491 (FJW 491), is approaching the sign for the Borough of

Bilston. Coming out of Moseley Road alongside the 1930s 'roadhouse'-styled George & Crown public house on the left is an AC three-wheeler invalid car, which, while it provided mobility, was an insult to the disabled, stigmatising them to a life of solo 'phutt-phutting' around in a two-stroke death-trap. On the right, the black car waiting at the entrance to Darlaston Lane is an early post-war Rover Ten; these were delightful to drive, but with its 25cwt six-light saloon body with only a 1389cc engine to drag it about, 65mph was hard work. *J. C. Brown*

Below left The section of the 25 route between Bilston and Willenhall was ideal for trolleybus operation with its long straight sections and long sweeping curves. Speeding along Bilston Street is 486 (FJW 486), an 8-foot-wide Park Royal-bodied Guy BT that entered service in June 1949. It is 23 April 1961, and 486 is looking quite smart despite being halfway between repaints. It is being followed by a Bedford O-type 5-ton lorry and an Austin Series 3 5-ton lorry, whose cab was designed and built by the Willenhall Motor Radiator Company, while in the distance are two trolleybuses bound for Bilston. The nearer lorry is passing St Thomas More Roman Catholic School on the left as a number of pupils circulate around the entrance; by 2003 the school site had become a new housing development. On the right is a row of terraced Victorian houses that are almost at the present-day site of the island over the new A454 Keyway. *J. C. Brown*

Above right The usual trolleybuses used latterly on the 25 service were Park Royal-bodied Guy BTs, which entered service during the summer and autumn of 1949. Here 484 (FJW 484) turns out of Rose Hill into Bilston Street on 18 March 1961. Behind it, outside the distinctive house on the

corner, is a black Morris Oxford V; today this house has gone, replaced by blocks of luxury low-height blocks of flats. To the right of 484 the 1930s houses continue along Bilston Lane towards the junction with Wolverhampton Road, which was traversed by the jointly operated 29 trolleybus route. *J. C. Brown*

Below Climbing the steep hill in Rose Hill, coming away from Willenhall station and approaching Tyler Road on the left on 21 April 1961, is 488 (FJW 488), a Guy BT with a Park Royal composite body. On a climb such as this, the trolleybus's 95hp BTH motor would have enabled the vehicle to easily out-perform a contemporary diesel-engined motor bus. Just visible at the bottom of the hill are the enclosed steps down to the platforms of Willenhall station. The parked Standard Vanguard Phase I on the left is outside the only row of Victorian houses between the railway station and Bilston Street. This area had been an area of coal-mining and clay pits, but after years of dereliction it became part of Willenhall's suburbia in the 1930s. *J. C. Brown*

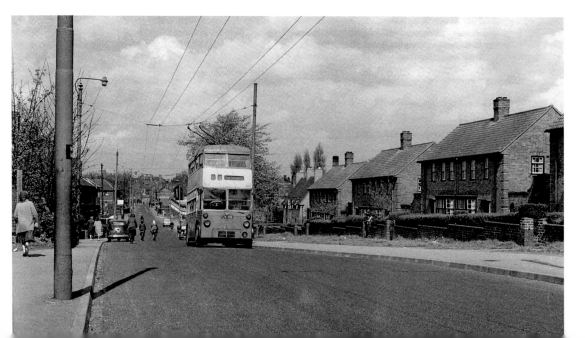

Above Having left the Willenhall terminus opposite the Market Place in New Road, the 25 service travelled southwards in Rose Hill before reaching Willenhall station, opened on 4 July 1837 as part of the original Grand Junction Railway. The trolleybus has just crossed the narrow Waterglade railway bridge over what, on 1 January 1846, had become part of the LNWR. The station closed in 1965, though the line was subsequently electrified and remains open today. Following Guy BT trolleybus 487 (FJW 487), on its way to Fighting Cocks, is a Morris J2 van. *J. C. Brown*

Below Although the 25 service was already doomed, the closure of Waterglade bridge for reconstruction as part of the West Coast Main Line electrification scheme led to the suspension of the 25 trolleybus route, and for the second time in four years Wolverhampton hired buses from Birmingham City Transport. This time Daimler CVD6s, rather than CVG6s, were hired, and the cost was met by British Railways. All that was required to keep the trolleybuses running was to put in a reverser at Rose Hill Gardens, opposite the Waterglade public house, using second-hand traction poles and wire retained from earlier abandonments. Eric Ball was in charge of overhead and electrical infrastructure for the

undertaking, and put forward cheap proposals to construct a new turning circle, but was over-ruled and trolleybus operation ceased. BCT 2003 (JOJ 3), a CVD6 with a Metro-Cammell H30/24R body, stands at the trolleybus stop in Rose Hill with the abruptly cut-off trolley wires hanging gauntly above its khaki-painted roof. In the background the brick and concrete rubble shows that work is well under way to demolish the offending bridge. *A. D. Broughall*

Above right The Willenhall terminus of the 25 service was at the bottom of Rose Hill, in Bilston Street. Here the trolleybuses unloaded alongside the ivy-covered Georgian Dale House, with its five bays and Adam-style doorway. The trolleybuses then crossed the wiring for the 29 trolleybus route, which was jointly worked by Wolverhampton and Walsall Corporations. The empty trolleybus then turned around the island where New Road, in the foreground, the Market Place and Walsall Street meet and returned to Rose Hill before waiting for departure time back to Fighting Cocks. Sunbeam W4 trolleybus 408 (DJW 938), which originally had a one-off Weymann wartime body but was rebodied in March 1952, begins the turn to return to the loading-up point. In the distance, alongside the Royal George public house in Walsall Street, on the 29 service, is Walsall Corporation's 310 (BDY 819), numerically the last of eight former Hastings Tramways Weymann-bodied Sunbeam W4s that were acquired by Walsall in June 1959. *J. C. Brown*

Right Having gone all the way around the island in the centre of Willenhall, the 25 trolleybus arrived at the terminus in Bilston Street where it waited until its timetabled departure time. The driver and the conductor, with his Ultimate ticket machine, stand alongside the sliding cab door of their charge, trolleybus 480 (FJW 480), a 1948 Park Royal-bodied Sunbeam F4. After the 25 service was closed on 26 October 1964, the joint service to

Walsall continued to operate through Willenhall until it too met an abrupt end on 31 October 1965, when building work on the M6 forced the route to close. Behind the trolleybus, beyond the Railway Tavern public house, a British Railways Dennis Pax lorry comes out of Walsall Street in front of the Royal George public house, while on the parking area opposite Rose Hill, next to the Market Place, is a parked four-door Austin A40 Devon. *D. F. Parker*

To Willenhall and Walsall

The comparatively flat route from Wolverhampton to Willenhall was operated by the Corporation's single-deck tramcars as far as the Market Place in Willenhall. The first section of the tram route, from Horseley Fields to Coventry Street, was opened on 2 April 1904 and further extended along Willenhall Road to Deans Road just three weeks later. As only single-deck tramcars could operate along Willenhall Road, and there was shortage of them in the Corporation's stock, three additional trams, numbered 41-43, were purchased from UEC in 1906. The Wolverhampton District Company contributed to the cost of these, and they were used when the through service to Willenhall Market Place began on 18 April 1906. The Willenhall Road tram route was totally converted to the overhead current collection method on 22 July 1921, but the state of the track deteriorated rapidly over the next few years. The lease on the line from Deans Road to the Market Place did not expire until the last month of 1927, but before then the Corporation bought the line from the Company, and on the day after it acquired the rights on 9 August 1926, buses were substituted between Wolverhampton and Willenhall Market Place.

The route through Horseley Fields passed through an area of heavy industry, making tubes, tools, castings and machine tools, before crossing James Brindley's Birmingham Canal, opened in 1772. The route then dived beneath the LNWR's Stour Valley line of 1852 and over the old OW&W railway bridge of 1854, which led to Wolverhampton's Low Level station. Once on to Willenhall Road, the service went through several areas of isolated Victorian terraces before reaching Stow Heath and its numerous coal mines and brickworks. Once through Moseley and Portobello, with its awkward bridge over the old Grand Junction Railway line, the route arrived in New Road, before terminating at the Market Place in the world-famous lock-making town of Willenhall. Once beyond Willenhall, the route entered Walsall territory (see Silver Link's *A Nostalgic Tour of Walsall by Tram, Trolleybus and Bus*, page 139).

The replacement 5 trolleybus service from the top of Horseley Fields at the Pipers Row junction to Neachells Lane was opened on 16 May 1927 and was extended through Portobello along High Street and into New Road to the old tram terminus at the Market Place exactly four months later, on 16 September 1927. The trolleybus route was suspended for more than six months from 27 April 1931 while the canal bridge over the Wolverhampton Level of the Birmingham Canal in Horseley Fields was rebuilt. The joint through working with Walsall Corporation beyond Willenhall to Walsall began on Monday 6 November 1931, after the roadway under the LNWR/LMS railway bridge in Lower Horseley Fields was lowered to accommodate the height of the new double-decker trolleybuses. The electricity for the joint service was supplied by Wolverhampton Corporation, to include the turning circle at Willenhall, so Walsall Corporation trolleybuses that turned short at the Market Place were charged a levy of 2s 6d per 100 shortworkings. It was at this turnback point that the 25 trolleybus terminated at Rose Hill.

The joint service was very successful, but the problems of congestion at the junction of Pipers Row and Horseley Fields led to a new terminus in St James's Square being brought into use in 1951 for the trolleybus service to Walsall. The through trolleybus service was closed prematurely on 31 October 1965 when the construction of the M6 motorway at Bentley prevented its continued operation.

The main bus routes that used or crossed Willenhall Road were the 42 service to New Invention via Willenhall, Neachells Lane, introduced on 2 December 1946, and the 45 to Bilston via Horseley Fields, Deans Road and Moseley Road, introduced on 6 November 1950, while the 72 route, introduced on 17 November 1958, turned off, with the 42 service, into Pinson

Road, just short of Willenhall, before crossing the suburbs and reaching Ashmore Park, by way,

originally, of a Bailey Bridge, giving the service access to the 1950s housing estate.

Right The original terminus of the 46 motorbus service to Warstones Estate was in St James's Square, but when it was extended across the town to the Underhill Estate, beyond Low Hill on the north side of Wolverhampton on 9 April 1951, the terminus was transferred to Railway Street. The buses travelled out of the town centre by way of Broad Street before turning left immediately beyond the railway bridge into Hilton Street. They then turned into Cannock Road before heading into the Low Hill and Underhill Estates, which were rapidly developing at this time. Brush-bodied Daimler CVG6 515 (FJW 515), dating from February 1950, stands in Railway Street, just beyond the Chubb Building, in the mid-1950s. *C. Carter*

Below The original Wolverhampton terminus of the jointly operated 29 service was at the top of Horseley Fields, but in order for the trolleybuses to turn round they had to enter the Five Ways end of Victoria Square. This manoeuvre was discontinued after 15 October 1951 when St James's Square was brought into operation. With the Victoria Hotel in the background, Walsall Corporation's 237 (JDH 434), a wartime Sunbeam W4 with a Roe semi-utility H30/26R body, which had entered service in March 1946, turns in front of the old entrance building to Wolverhampton High Level station, which has survived to the present day. It is about to return to Horseley Fields, where it will stop outside the loading-up shelters. A Wolverhampton Corporation Brush-bodied Daimler CVG6 passes in front of Berry Street on the left, while coming from Railway Street on its journey from Bloxwich on the 60 service is a Walsall Leyland 'Titan' PD2/1 with an unusually styled Park Royal composite body, built specially to the specification of Mr M. J. Somerfield, the General Manager. *J. Hughes*

Top The original terminus of the 5 route was in Horseley Fields opposite the Station Garage with its attractive Cleveland, Power and Shell petrol globes. The garage was owned by Bertie Hopcutt Jnr, a colourful local character who was an agent for Bentley and Jaguar cars. In 1950, barely two years old, is trolleybus 458 (FJW 458), a Sunbeam F4 with a Park Royal H28/26R body. The original livery of these trolleybuses was green and yellow with two thin black livery lines between the decks, a dark matt grey painted roof and shaded gold fleet numbers. All this conspired to make the buses look extremely smart and bright in the frequently dingy industrial environment of early postwar Wolverhampton. The Willenhall route had been partially opened to Neachells Lane on 16 May 1927, with a terminus in Horseley Fields. As already mentioned, the trolleybuses originally had the terminus turn-back wiring across the Pipers Row junction, but after 15 October 1951 these were removed when the terminus was moved to St James's Square, by which time the route, jointly worked with Walsall, had been in operation for a month short of 20 years. *A. B. Cross*

Middle After the closure of the 29 trolleybus route, the replacement 29 buses had a much larger seating capacity. In early 1966 Guy 'Arab' V 102 (7102 UK) is turning out of Union Street into Little Park Street, which led into St James's Square. The bus was bodied by Weymann with an H41/31F seating capacity and entered service in June 1963 in preparation for the decimation of the trolleybus services later that year. Many of Wolverhampton's old domestic premises had been converted many years before into industrial use, but had now reached the end of their lives and were virtually derelict; 102 is alongside such a building. The tall factory building on the right was latterly used by the Wolverhampton amateur boxing club. In the background is Horseley Fields, while parked in Union Street is a Hillman Super Minx Series II, first registered in February 1963. *A. D. Broughall*

Bottom Looking across St James's Square we can see the route that the trolleybuses took from the distant Little Park Street to gain access to the terminus bus stop alongside the wall of Walsall Street School. Pulling away from those stops on 7 May 1961 is

trolleybus 620 (FJW 620), a Sunbeam F4 fitted with an 8-foot-wide Park Royal H28/26R body that entered service on 25 March 1949. Behind it is Walsall Corporation's 850 (HBE 541), one of the few Crossley 'Empire' TDD42/3s chassis not to be operated by Manchester City Transport. It was built in 1950 for Grimsby-Cleethorpes as its No 63 and, with its elegant Charles Roe H29/25R body, was acquired by Walsall, entering service in February 1961. By this time St James's Square had lost many of its surrounding buildings and had degenerated into an area ripe for redevelopment. However, it gave the trolleybuses a usefully quiet turning circle by way of the separate roads in and out of it. *J. C. Brown*

Top The 42 service also had its town terminus in St James's Square. This route, introduced on 29 July 1949, followed Willenhall Road as far as Pinson Road, before heading north by way of Stubby Lane and Lichfield Road to the new housing estates that were developing in New Invention. One of the first 30-foot-long buses, 29 (YDA29), a Guy 'Arab' IV with a full-front Metro-Cammell 'Orion' H41/31F body, which had been delivered in January 1960, is in St James's Square, in company with a parked Ford Zephyr EOTTA, a Ford Anglia E93A, an early post-war Morris 10 Series M, and a Ford Consul II 204E in the centre of the square. *D. R. Harvey collection*

Middle About to turn into Union Street from Horseley Fields are two Wolverhampton trolleybuses. The leading vehicle, 442 (EJW 442), is on the 29 service from Walsall; with its Sunbeam W4 chassis, it entered service on 10 May 1947 with a post-war-styled Park Royal H28/26R body, but was rebodied by Charles Roe in August 1960. Behind it is another trolleybus from the same batch, on the 5 route from Willenhall. The old building on the corner of Union Street is the premises of Electrical Conduits, which supplied cabling, conduits and jointing to electrical contractors in the building trade. The out-of-town overhead for the 29 service continued down Horseley Fields, but after 1951 the trolleybuses used Union Street in order to reach the terminus in St James's Square, the wiring towards Piper's Row only being used for depot workings. On the left, turning to travel along Horseley Fields, lined with Victorian developments, is an Austin A40 Farina. *R. F. Mack*

Bottom The driver of Park Royal-bodied Guy BT 632 (FJW

632) has already turned his destination blind for the return journey as he drives along Horseley Fields, passing Mary Ann Street on the left. The next side street on the left was Gough Street, followed by Union Street, into which the trolleybus will turn. On the left are the pillars of the Mount Zion Methodist Chapel, which dated from the early years of Queen Victoria's reign, while opposite the trolleybus is a row of early Victorian premises converted to shops. *D. R. Harvey collection*

Left Travelling along Horseley Fields in about 1968, passing the 1950s telephone exchange with the Mount Zion Methodist Chapel in the background, is Guy 'Arab' V 199 (MDA 199E), working on the 5 route as far as Willenhall. It has a Strachan H41/31F body, which at first sight looks like a product of Washwood Heath – alas, not the case. Wolverhampton stuck to the format of front engines with pre-selector gearboxes and forward-entrance bodies virtually until the end. The largest Black Country brewery, Banks's, is based in Wolverhampton, and its highly recommended beers have been called 'cheap and cheerful', thus having only one similarity with the body contracts for some of the later buses – the Strachan bodies were just cheap! The MDA-registered batch first entered service in January 1967 in advance of the abandonment of the final trolleybus route to Dudley, yet by 1972 some of the worst examples had shaken themselves into withdrawal, despite being barely five years old! Following the bus along Horseley Fields is an eight-wheeled Albion 'Caledonian' 24C/5 oil-tanker with a lightweight cab built in fibre-glass by Alfred Miles of Gloucester in 1959, which featured a distinctive forward-sloping windscreen. *A. J. Douglas*

Below left Horseley Fields, as far as about Shakespeare Street, was lined with old domestic premises, many of which had been converted into small workshops, factories or warehouses. It was at this point that the main road turned due east, and it was here in tramway days that the first passing loop outside the town centre was laid as the slight bend enabled the carriageway to be a little wider. Parked in front of Zinc Alloy Rust Proofing on the right is a Standard 10 saloon and an NSU Prinz III registered in Renfrew during the summer of 1962 – it would have been a brave driver who would have come all the way from Scotland in this tiny rear-engined 583cc four-seater (in fact, it belonged to the photographer, Cliff Brown!) At the end of the 1960s NSU built cars with the Wankel rotary engine, which was very advanced, theoretically brilliant, but dreadfully frail and unreliable. The company eventually sold out to the re-

emerging Audi company, which had begun to manufacture cars again in 1966; by 1977 NSU and its version of the Wankel engine were no more, though the rotary engine is still successfully produced by Mazda. On the left is the imposing factory of Tools (Wolverhampton) Ltd, industrial tool manufacturers, while roughly where the Austin A55 is are the premises of T. & C. Clark, makers of vitreous enamel hollow-ware and water-fittings for the plumbing industry. Beyond the distant canal bridge on the skyline are the foundry chimneys of Qualcast's Crane Works and the outbuildings along the company's canal-side wharf. These works had been taken over in 1945 from the Crane Foundry Company, which also made castings for the motor trade, cookers and lawnmowers. The canal bridge takes Horseley Fields over the Wolverhampton Level of the Birmingham Canal, opened in 1772 at a water level of 473 feet. *J. C. Brown*

Below On the 5 shortworking to Willenhall and passing beneath Horseley Fields bridge is 411 (DJW 941), a Sunbeam W4 chassis that entered service on 5 May 1945. Behind it is a recently rebodied Sunbeam W4 with its more powerful Metrovick BTH 85hp motor, which is going all the way to Walsall. When the 402-417 series trolleybuses were rebodied in 1952 with Park Royal H28/26R bodies, their appearance must have been a disappointment as they were virtually the same as those originally fitted in 1948 to the trolleybus behind. This route was originally operated by single-deckers using Tilling-Stevens TS6 vehicles dating from between the end of 1923 and the beginning of 1926. After much wrangling with the LMS, successor to the LNWR, the bridge was lowered, closing the trolleybus route between 27 April and 7 November 1931. It resumed just nine days before the through working with Walsall Corporation was due to begin; the railed, raised pavement shows the original height of the road. Passing over the bridge is English Electric diesel-electric Type 4 1Co-Co1 No D221, named *Ivernia* after a Cunard passenger liner. It has come from Euston and is travelling the last few yards into Wolverhampton High Level station. *A. B. Cross*

Below Passing along Lower Horseley Fields towards Wolverhampton on the 45 route from Prouds Lane, Bilston, and Moseley Road is bus 12 (SUK 12), a Guy 'Arab' IV with a Metro-Cammell 'Orion' H33/27R body. It was delivered in May 1957, one of six fitted with a Gardner 6LW engine, and would survive long enough to be transferred to the WMPTE, being finally withdrawn in 1973. It is passing James Summerhill's early post-war office block; the company was established in 1877 and manufactured corrugated aluminium, alloy and steel sheet under the name of Beaver Star Brand. Parked outside the office block is a Ford Zephyr 6 Mk III dating from May 1963 – remember BBC TV's Z Cars? *A. B. Cross*

Bottom On Tuesday 30 March 1948, working into Wolverhampton in Willenhall Road, is 349 (BJW 149), a Daimler COG5 with a Brush H29/25R body built in 1938. It is operating on the 42 service from Neachells Lane and is passing a Victorian terrace near Colliery Road, which was the home of Herbertson & Co, manufacturer of steel-framed buildings, roofs and riveted girders at its Beaconsfield Works. The 42 route had originally been introduced on 2 December 1946 to Neachells Lane and Deans Road by way of Willenhall Road, and was only extended to the Gate Inn,

New Invention, on 29 July 1949, effectively doubling its length. No 349, fitted with 'utility' seating in the upper saloon, would be withdrawn in 1952, although seven of the 340-351 class, the last pre-war motorbuses to be delivered, lasted until 1957. *F. W. Shuttleworth*

Right A distant single-decker tram, one of the 37-43 class of UEC closed combination cars, is coming out of Wolverhampton towards Willenhall near the junction on the right with Old Heath Road. By this time the route had been converted from the Lorain Surface Contact stud system to overhead current collection, although the studs are still visible on the road. This conversion had taken place on 22 July 1921 and the tram route (6) had closed on 8 August 1926. On the left in Willenhall Road are the Edwardian terraces and inevitable shop that occupied the corner of Plascom Road, which led to East Park, opened in 1896 on derelict industrial land given to the town by its owners, the Duke of Sutherland and Sir Alfred Hickman. If it didn't have quite the social cachet of West Park, it provided a boating lake (which had an early propensity to drain away into the underlying former colliery workings), a bandstand, a quickly abandoned lido and tree-lined walks with large tracts of open grassland in between. In an area of heavy industry and mining, East Park provided a lung of greenery in an otherwise fairly bleak industrial district. On the right, in Willenhall Road, is the British Oak public house on the corner of Coventry Street. This had been the original Corporation tram terminus, opened on 2 April 1904; the through Corporation service to Willenhall began on 18 April 1906. Parked outside the pub is a Coventry-manufactured Swift 10hp open tourer built in about 1922. *J. Hughes collection*

Right Just before the Deans Road junction in Willenhall Road was Tyburn Road, where the Rydal Green flat development was built to replace an early Victorian housing area packed into a cramped triangle of land that had running through it Chapel Street, Cross Street and Dark Street. On the extreme left is a large 1950s house that was used as a doctor's surgery, while off the picture is the future site of the Mayfield Housing Estate; the wide road space will be left for future road widening. Originally the Wolverhampton District Electric Tramways owned the section of track between Deans Road and Willenhall and operated a shuttle service between those two points until it was taken over by the Corporation as a through service in 1906. Around the corner was located a Mercury-Arc Rectifier power sub-station, which supplied the electric overhead as far as Willenhall. After the Fighting Cocks to Willenhall service was closed on 26 October 1964, hired Birmingham Daimler CVD6s were occasionally put to work on the 5 route along Willenhall Road as far as Market Place, Willenhall.

One of them, HOV 952 of 1949 with an MCCW H30/24R body, overtakes an Austin A40 as it passes the Rydal Green flats and approaches the large Merry Boys public house, built in the 1960s in the angle between Willenhall Road and Deans Road to serve the area's new housing developments. Opposite is the north end of Stow Heath Lane, where the Corporation's original tramway electricity supply ended and that of the Company operation began. *A. B. Cross*

Below Immediately after the junction at the Merry Boys public house, and with Deans Road left behind, the trolleybus route quickly reached the junction with Neachells Lane. Travelling along Willenhall Road on 3 October 1965 working on the 5 route shortworking from Willenhall is 8-foot-wide Park Royal-bodied Guy BT 498 (FJW 498), passing Moseley Road on the right with Harrison's Mini Market on the corner. It is following an Austin A40 Devon, while peeping out of Neachells Lane on the left, in front of the Neachells public house, is a Mark II Jaguar. In the distance are the low factory

office buildings of Edmund Vaughan Stampings, while on the skyline can be made out the multi-storey flats at Portobello, awaiting demolition in 2003. *J. C. Brown*

Bottom Coasting over the feeder point in Willenhall Road, and passing the entrance to Noose Lane on the right, is 638 (FJW 638), a 1949 Guy BT trolleybus with an 8-foot-wide Park Royal H28/26R body, working on the 29 service to Walsall during April 1961. When the Wednesfield trolleybus service was abandoned on 3 November 1963, this vehicle

would be withdrawn. Subsequently all but one of these Guys and the Sunbeam W4s were withdrawn on 8 August 1965 after the abandonment of the 2 and 7 routes between Darlaston and Whitmore Reans; strangely, 478 (FJW 478), the last trolleybus to be repainted, survived until 25 October 1965, just a week before the closure of the jointly worked Walsall trolleybus service. About 200 yards away along Noose Lane, beyond the long-established timber yard on the corner, is a level crossing on the former LNWR main line. Following the trolleybus is a Humber Hawk Mark II, which, with its wrap-around windscreen, looks like an American compact car. *J. C. Brown*

Above right Wolverhampton's last tramcar was 69, the last of the eight Brush-built single-deckers that were copies of the front-entrance tramcars developed by the Birmingham & Midland Tramway Company at its Tividale Works in 1919; it was

delivered to the undertaking in the spring of 1922. This type of four-wheeled 32-seater tram was a last-ditch attempt to keep tramcars profitable in the Black Country, especially where routes were lightly loaded. It is crossing the former LNWR main line at Portobello on its way from Willenhall towards Wolverhampton. The late-Victorian terraced houses in the background are on the corner of High Street, the main road, and Dilloway's Lane. Portobello was named after the naval battle at Porto Bello, on the Isthmus of Darien, Panama, which took place on 22 November 1739 when the British naval fleet led by Admiral Edward Vernon, whose family came from nearby Essington, sacked the town. Portobello was developed in the 18th century as an area renowned for its brick-making, though coal-mining predominated in the following century. *J. Hughes collection*

Below On a quiet Sunday 3 October 1965, trolleybus 443 (EJW 443), a 1947 Sunbeam W4 that re-entered service with a new Roe H32/28R body on 7 February 1962, having been out of service for almost 12 months, speeds along an almost deserted New Road, Willenhall. Working on the 29 service, it has just passed the Castle Inn on the corner of Peel Street, Willenhall's second oldest pub, dating from the early 19th century, when it had been a coaching inn. Beyond that, about ten buildings away towards Portobello, is the site of the Lock Museum, which shows the heritage of the town exemplified by this Victorian locksmith's house and workshop. The billboard on the near derelict row of mid-19th-century houses shows that the Dale Cinema, located on the corner of New Road and Bilston Street, in the centre of Willenhall, is showing the Beatles in Dick Lester's film *Help*. *J. C. Brown*

Top In pouring rain, 411 (DJW 941), a Park Royal-rebodied wartime Sunbeam W4, on its last day in service, leaves the Market Place, Willenhall, with the distant white-painted Royal George public house in the background, where the Fighting Cocks trolleybuses terminated in Bilston Street. The trolleybus is travelling along New Road and is passing what would have been a very fine Victorian semi-detached villa, but by this time is the premises of the Westminster Bank. It is working on the 29 route in October 1965, which was when the service finally closed, and is being followed by an Austin A60 and a minivan. The parked cars being passed are a Ford Cortina 113E two-door saloon first registered in November 1963 and a Ford Consul II 204E dating from about 1960. *D. R. Harvey collection*

Middle and bottom The terminus of the Willenhall tram route was in New Road, Willenhall, at the junction with the Market Place and Bilston Street; the tall Midland Bank building on the right is on the corner of Market Place and New Road. In the right foreground is a facing cross-over that was used by Walsall Corporation trams coming from that town. Just in front of the tram is the curve from Bilston Street into New Road, part of the Wolverhampton District tram service that was a section of the circular working from Bilston to Darlaston; it was also the connection to the Willenhall to Dean's Road service. Trams working on the circular service had to reverse here because the connection only turned towards Wolverhampton. Sunday 8 August 1926 was the last day of operation on the Willenhall 6 tram route, meaning that these neat little tramcars only operated on this route for just over four years. The Company circular service ceased on 30 November 1928, though the section of the Willenhall service as far as Crescent Road, operated by Walsall Corporation, was not abandoned until 4 February 1929. After the tram abandonments, trolleybuses from Wolverhampton began working through to Willenhall on 16 September 1927 after a year of motorbus operation, while Walsall Corporation began a single-deck bus service after its tram route closure. Walsall Corporation was cajoled to introduce a joint trolleybus service, and eventually agreed to purchase trolleybuses. Even then, they had to be double-deckers, so it was only after the lowering of the Horseley Fields railway bridge that the through service was introduced on 16 November 1931.

Waiting at the bus layover in Walsall Street on 30 April 2001, adjacent to

the Royal George public house, is Travel West Midlands Dennis 'Trident' 4141, (Y735 TOH), fitted with an Alexander H47/28F body. The bus is working on the 529 service to Walsall, and has only been in service for four weeks – the bus route that replaced the trolleybuses was renumbered by the WMPTE in 1969 by simply adding 500 to the existing route number. Today, the buildings in the now pedestrianised Market Place, to the right of the turreted HSBC bank and behind the bus, have survived as an oasis of low-rise Victorian development. Willenhall was the home of the English lock-making industry, with the two premier lock manufacturers, Josiah Parkes and Yale. Even today there are 15 listed lock manufacturers based here. *D. R. Harvey collection/D. R. Harvey*

territory. In the background the Dale Cinema is showing the 1961 film *Weekend With Lulu*, starring the late Bob Monkhouse and Shirley Eaton. The cinema is now a public house called the Malthouse. *J. C. Brown*

Above right Women drivers! When a trolleybus was de-wired, the driver usually had a look of 'It won't me, mate', but when one of Walsall's lady drivers managed this feat in the middle of Willenhall, it was a rare occurrence to capture the moment on film. Walsall Corporation's 304 (BDY 808) was attempting to turn around at the junction with Bilston Street in the middle of Willenhall during July 1961. This former Hastings Tramways 33, a 95hp Sunbeam W4, was built with a Weymann H30/26R body, entering service in September 1947 and acquired by Walsall in June 1959; it survived until 16 February 1970, when nearly all the short-length trolleybuses were withdrawn with the first stage of trolleybus abandonment. The splitting point on the overhead wiring near the Parish Church was where power supplies between Wolverhampton and Walsall met, and every Walsall trolleybuses turning short at Willenhall was charged 2s 6d for every 100 of these manoeuvres into 'enemy'

Below Turning in the opposite direction, back into New Road, is Roe-rebodied Sunbeam W4 trolleybus 432 (DUK 832). It is on the shortworking 5 service on 31 October 1965, the last day of the joint trolleybus service, and is returning to Wolverhampton. To the right of the Midland Bank, with its curious steeple, is the Market Place; unlike many other Black Country towns, Willenhall has managed to retain many of its original 19th-century buildings, and all of those visible have survived to the present day. In the foreground is the former terminus of the Fighting Cocks route in Bilston Street, whose forced closure had occurred a year earlier. All the overhead has been dismantled in Bilston Street and it wouldn't be too long before the 29 route wiring would be brought down. *A. B. Cross*

Below Willenhall in the 1920s was a town devoted to lock-making, though its industrial past of poor living conditions derived from the poorly paid coal-miners and clay-pit workers. The lock-making industry is represented on the right by the Triumph Works of Lester & Parton, motor lock-makers located at the back of 84 Walsall Street, typically little more than a downstairs domestic industry. Travelling from the Bull Stake at Darlaston towards the Market Place in Walsall Street during 1925 is Wolverhampton District single-decker tramcar 109, one of the nine cars purchased by the company between 1919 and 1920 to enable it to compete with the ever increasing numbers of both independent bus operators and, ironically, its own BET owners! These modern 32-seaters were mounted on Tividale-built 8ft 6in trucks, but wooden longitudinal seats were a distinctly old-fashioned feature. No 109 was the penultimate car built for Wolverhampton District, having the second highest fleet number of any tram in the Black Country. It has passed a man leading a white shire horse near the present-day County

public house, and will take the reversing loop in Market Place into Bilston Street. *D. R. Harvey collection*

Bottom In Walsall Street the trolleybuses coming from Walsall had a lay-by to stand in so that other traffic could overtake them. The lay-by was outside the impressive Victorian Gothic Parish Church of St Giles; dating from 1867, it was designed by W. D. Griffin, an architect based in nearby Wolverhampton who also designed St Stephen's Church at the other end of the town. On the left is Leve Lane and beyond that Doctor's Piece, near where the medieval Old Hall was located. One of its last occupants was Dr Richard Wilkes, who donated the land to the town in 1849; it was used as a burial ground for 211 of the 292 people who succumbed to the cholera epidemic of that year. On 10 October 1965 trolleybus 427 (DUK 827), a wartime Sunbeam W rebodied by Roe in 1959, drifts into the lay-by when working on the 29 service. To the right of the following Ford Prefect is St Giles C of E School, while on the distant bend is the Prince of Wales public house. *J. C. Brown*

Right Pulling up at the trolleybus stop in Walsall Road opposite Fisher Street on the left is 438 (EJW 438). This 1947-built Sunbeam W4 had been rebodied by Charles Roe in May 1960, and is working on the 29 service to Walsall on 10 October 1965. The houses in this part of eastern Willenhall, near Shepwell Green, dated from the late 1880s, but were still mixed in with the lock-making industry. On the left is the Acorn pub, which still trades today; it is near the site of John Harper's Albion Works, founded in 1790 as one of the earliest and subsequently largest lock-makers in the town. Just visible at the Willenhall end

of Walsall Road is the half-timbered Old Toll House, while parked in front of the greengrocer's shop is a Ford Thames 307E 7cwt van; these had been introduced in 1961 as the commercial version of the Ford Anglia. *J. C. Brown*

Below right Armstrong Stevens, located on the corner of Walsall Road and Clarkes Lane, were drop forgers who manufactured the well-known Lion Brand of wrenches and spanners, and were one of Willenhall's larger employers. The factory was sufficiently important to warrant its own bus shelter, though these desperate corrugated-covered scaffolding structures offered little protection. In the foreground is Crescent Road, which was used by Company cars on the circular service from Darlaston. The trolleybus crossing the traffic lights on its way to Wolverhampton is Roe-rebodied Sunbeam W 449 (EJW 449); it entered service on New Year's Day 1948 with a Park Royal composite body that had echoes of wartime designs. It was withdrawn for rebodying in mid-December 1960 and, with its replacement body, lasted until the final closure of the system on 5 March 1967. On leaving Clarkes Lane,

the road to Walsall crossed the infant River Tame at County Bridge before climbing the hill towards Bentley. On the way the road crossed the Bentley Canal, built in 1843 as a 3 mile 3 furlong short cut between Wolverhampton and the Walsall branch of the Birmingham Canal; it was officially abandoned in 1961, the same year that 449 came back into service with its new body. *J. C. Brown*

Above Near what is now Junction 10 of the M6, the present-day Wolverhampton Road West looks a little wider but the buildings are the same. At the distant junction with the traffic lights is the 1950s Lane Arms public house on the extreme right, on the corner of Bentley Mill Way. On the left of Queen Elizabeth Avenue are some council-built maisonettes and houses, which also date from the early post-war years. The trolleybus, 427 (DUK 827), is about to begin the long descent down to the Bentley Canal just under half a mile away. The Sunbeam W4, being overtaken by an MG Midget, is one of the 38 that were rebodied by Charles Roe between 1958 and 1962. *J. C. Brown*

Below Beyond the present-day M6 motorway junction at Bentley, whose construction was the prime reason for the closure of the jointly worked 29 trolleybus route, the trolleybuses crossed Anson Bridge over the Anson Branch of the BCN's Walsall canal system, work on which began in 1840. Behind the trees on the left are the distant cooling towers of Birchills Power Station in Green Lane, built by the West Midlands Joint Electricity Authority prior to the industry being nationalised on 1 April 1948. These were demolished in the 1990s. Trolleybus 446 (EJW 446), a Sunbeam W4 of 1947 and rebodied by Roe in January 1962, is speeding past Bloxwich Lane, causing it to heel over as it takes the curve in

Wolverhampton Road and across the boundary into Walsall where the line of inter-war housing begins. No 446 had already been used as the last trolleybus to Wednesfield in November 1963, and was destined to be used on the last trolleybus tour to Walsall. It was kept in Bilston depot after the final closure in March 1967 as a possible preservation candidate, but in the event was used only for spares for 433 (DUK 833), which is still the 'baby' of one of the authors. A feature of Walsall's trolleybus wiring was the use of side overhead feeder wires, which are attached to the far-side traction poles. *J. C. Brown*

Right   Coming out of Walsall in Wolverhampton Road on the last day of the 29 route's operation, 31 October 1965, 434 (EJW 434), the first of the 1947 batch of Sunbeam W4s rebodied by Roe in 1960, has just begun to drop down the gentle gradient into the town, which started here, near Raleigh

Street – today this stretch of road is a wide dual-carriageway with speed cameras and parking restrictions. The old cottages on the right, with compulsory demolition notices on their walls, as well as many of the later Victorian terraces, have gone, though nearer to the Pleck Road junction, the Orange Tree public house and the old Board junior school premises have survived. Following the trolleybus is a Morris 1100 and a Karrier Gamecock owned by GPO Telephones, while in the distance a Walsall Corporation trolleybus travels eastwards towards Willenhall. *J. C. Brown*

Below   Having crossed the junction with Pleck Road,

Wolverhampton Street immediately crossed the BCN's Walsall Canal at Canal Street; the iron railings of the bridge are to the right of the trolleybus, while a Ford Zephyr 206E turns from Pleck Road on the left. The trolleybus is once again 432 (DUK 832), a Roe-rebodied Sunbeam W4 that was to see service until March 1967. The impressive building dominating this section of Wolverhampton Street is the Albion Flour Mill constructed in 1848, with canalside access. Lamentably, in 2003 this fine example of a mid-19th-century industrial building lies derelict. Just visible is the top deck of one of Walsall Corporation's low-height Willowbrook-bodied Daimler CVG6s of 1956. *J. C. Brown*

Above On 31 October 1965, the last day of operation, the 29 trolleybus service was being jointly operated as usual by both Corporations. It was a miserable Sunday, as the brightness of the illuminated Regent petrol station sign shows; this garage, where the Ford Anglia is about to be filled up with petrol, was at the junction of Wolverhampton Street West and Blue Lane West. The Walsall trolleybus and Willowbrook-bodied forward-entrance bus are both taking the right fork into Wolverhampton Street towards the distant ABC Cinema at the junction with Park Street, and are being followed by a speeding Austin A35 van. The Walsall trolleybus is 346 (ADX 195), a 1950 Sunbeam F4 with a Park Royal H30/26R body that was very similar to the FJW-registered Wolverhampton trolleybuses; it had been purchased from Ipswich Corporation in February 1962, where it had carried the fleet number 125. Coming out of Walsall on the 29 route is Roe-rebodied Sunbeam W4 trolleybus 440 (EJW 440). *J. C. Brown*

Below left The original Walsall terminus of the 29 service, which was used after Monday 16 November 1931, was at the top of Park Street in front of Her Majesty's Theatre. Here a turning circle was put in across the entrance of Green Lane and Stafford Street, and this lasted until 1950, when the trolleybuses were routed around the Savoy Cinema, which had replaced the old theatre in 1936. Immediately before the introduction of the loop around the picture house, the driver of trolleybus 650 (FJW 650), a Guy BT with a Park Royal 8-foot-wide H28/26R body that had entered service on 30 March 1950, hauls his charge round to the pick-up point outside the premises of the Warwickshire Furniture Company, just above the impressive Red Lion public house. In the background is the overhead in Green Lane already under construction above the Walsall bus for the re-positioning of the 29 terminus in Townend Street. *J. S. Webb*

months on Wolverhampton's remaining route to Sedgley and Dudley, being involved in an accident at Fighting Cocks on 14 January 1966. *J. C. Brown*

Below After the trolleybus abandonment in October 1965, the usual type of Wolverhampton Corporation motor bus used on the 29 service was the forward-entrance Guy 'Arab' V. Here the bus working on what was still a jointly operated service is 161 (GJW 161C), which entered service in August 1965 with a Weymann H41/31F body. It is turning into Townend Street from Green Lane at the rear of the ABC cinema. On the left is Richmond's kitchenware shop, which occupied the rounded corner site with Stafford Street, and in the background is Park Street, which led to the centre of Walsall town centre at The Bridge. *R. F. Mack*

Above Again on the last day, turning in front of the ABC Cinema in Park Street, a trolleybus comes out of Wolverhampton Street, turning across Park Street and into Green Lane on the right. The photographer, the late Cliff Brown, is standing roughly where the original terminus of the 29 service, abandoned in 1950, was located. The ABC is showing the 1965 western *The Sons of Katie Elder*, starring John Wayne and Dean Martin. Today the site of the cinema is occupied by a large Woolworth store, while to the extreme left in Wolverhampton Street is the new, impressive Walsall Art Gallery. No 430 (DUK 830), a Sunbeam W4 rebodied by Charles Roe in 1959, would survive for only a few more

Above After 1950, the ABC Cinema acted as a terminal loop for the 29 route, though typically for trolleybuses it was not on the main road, but tucked around the corner in an obscure side street. Parked in Townend Street off Green Lane when still quite new is 630 (FJW 630), the very last Sunbeam trolleybus bought new by the undertaking. Fitted with the usual 8-foot-wide Park Royal body, this Sunbeam F4 was one of four trolleybuses of this class to enter service on 2 May 1950, which also made them the last new trolleybuses to enter service with Wolverhampton Corporation. This was almost a month after the last Guy BT, 654, numerically also the last trolleybus, was put on to the road. The trolleybus has the trolleybase shrouds on the roof, which improved the look of the vehicle enormously. *D. R. Harvey collection*

Below On leaving the terminus, the trolleybuses went to the end of Townend Street where they followed the curve of the street behind the ABC Cinema before turning back into Wolverhampton Street and returning to Willenhall. To the left is the local warehouse of W. H. Smith, the bookseller and stationer. Also on the left is a Standard Ensign, first registered in Walsall in November 1961; this was a four-cylinder version of the Vanguard, but barely 20,000 were made. The trolleybus, 488 (FJW 488), a Guy BT with a Park Royal H28/26R body, has just left the Townend Street terminus bus shelters as it starts out on the long run to Wolverhampton. *R. Wellings*

To Wednesfield and Bloxwich

The route to Wednesfield and beyond passed through long rows of Victorian terraces that lined Wednesfield Road. Having left the town by Canal (latterly known as Broad) Street, the passenger became immediately aware of the necessity of using single-deckers, as the road took a deep plunge beneath the railway bridge that took traffic in and out of Wolverhampton High Level station. This bridge had been much enlarged throughout the 19th century since its original construction in 1852, but its headroom was still only 10ft 6in, which, though adequate for the horse and cart traffic, was a distinct limitation to the passenger-carrying capacity of both electric single-deck trams and the succeeding trolleybuses. Despite the privations of the Second World War, work began on lowering the roadway beneath the bridge in September 1943, with a £6,000 grant from the Ministries of War Transport and Supply. This was the last of the three railway bridges, in Stafford Road, Cannock Road and Wednesfield Road, which had bedevilled access to the north and east of the town, to be lowered. Two-way double-decker operation of trolleybuses began under the bridge on 17 February 1944.

Once free of the bridge the route passed the impressive entrance to the Great Western Railway's Wolverhampton Low Level station and forecourt before heading off to Heath Town. This former Urban District had been absorbed into Wolverhampton in 1927, but the Victorian housing, churches, schools and factories remained unaltered by the time the trams arrived. Although independent for many years, Heath Town was the first self-contained suburb along Wednesfield Road. It was in many ways a piece of municipal spite when the 1960s Heath Town redevelopment scheme destroyed the street layout there and replaced it with avant-garde multi-storey flats, maisonettes and 'walkways-in-the-sky', which due to dereliction and vandalism have had to be heavily modified to meet the demands of the early 21st century.

Climbing out of Heath Town, the road ran parallel to the BCN's Wyrley & Essington Canal of 1797, passing on its northern side Heath Town Park, laid out formally in 1920, before New Cross Hospital was reached. This had been the Wolverhampton Union Workhouse and dated from 1903, becoming a hospital in the 1920s; today it is the main A & E Hospital for the City of Wolverhampton. Beyond Rookery Bridge was Wednesfield, which was absorbed by its 'big brother' in 1966, though it still retains a separate and distinctive nature. Famous for its locks, keys and traps (for fox, rat and man!), Wednesfield was the last built-up area on the Lichfield Road before Bloxwich. Until the early 1950s most of the land to the east of Wednesfield on the road to Bloxwich was either undeveloped or still largely farmland, with virtually no primary or manufacturing industry.

The single-deck tram service on the Corporation's Lorain system was opened to Church Street, Heath Town, on 22 June 1904 and extended to New Street, Wednesfield, on 31 October of the same year. The trams were intended to go into Wednesfield's High Street under the terms of the authorisation under Tramway No 2 of the 1904 Wolverhampton Act, but the necessity to rebuild Rookery Bridge over the Wyrley & Essington Canal resulting in this section never being completed. The tram service, numbered 5, was converted to overhead operation on 28 July 1921 and was abandoned just 51 weeks later, because of the need to replace the worn-out tracks.

The Wednesfield route then became the pioneering trolleybus service in Wolverhampton, being opened on 29 October 1923 using six Tilling-Stevens TS6 central-entrance 40-seater single-deckers bodied by Christopher Dodson of Willesden. For the first time the new trolleybuses, running from a new terminus in Broad Street but retaining the route number 6, actually traversed the High Street in Wednesfield, terminating at the Dog & Partridge public house at Pinfold Bridge to the north of the town. A short extension to serve the late-1920s housing that had developed around Wood End Road was opened on 10 February 1934, where it met the 20 route from Bushbury Hill and Willenhall. As housing continued to be developed along and off Lichfield Road in the mid-1950s, and the large Wednesfield High School campuses were built, so the need for a further extension became a priority. On 10 January 1955 Wolverhampton's penultimate trolleybus extension was brought into use, partially using materials bought from the recently abandoned Birmingham CT tram system. The trolleybus extension of approximately a mile, agreed under the terms of the 1936 Wolverhampton Corporation Act, was not begun until the mid-1950s, when funds at last became available to widen Lichfield Road, when the surrouding area was being developed as a

municipal housing estate. The extension, briefly operated by motorbuses from 1 March 1954, went as far as the 1950s-built Albion Inn, which stands at the corner of Stubby Lane and opposite Linthouse Lane. Given the route number 59, the route closed on 3 November 1963.

On 9 May 1949 a new bus service was introduced, numbered 60 and operating over the existing trolleybus route to Wednesfield before heading cross-country to Bloxwich, representing another example of joint operation between Wolverhampton and Walsall Corporations. A number of motorbus routes either crossed or followed Wednesfield Road, including the 50, between Willenhall and Wednesfield, and various services into the Linthouse Lane and Ashmore Park housing estates, such as the 71.

Left When the Wednesfield route was converted from tramcar to trolleybus operation it was only the second time in the country that such a conversion had taken place. Wolverhampton's first trolleybuses were six Tilling-Stevens TS6s with BTH 50hp motors and Dodson B40C bodies, and were numbered 1 to 6. The first trolleybus, registered DA 7741, was licensed on the day of the opening of the trolleybus system, Monday 29 October 1923. A centre-entrance single-decker with 'stick-thin' wooden window pillars, it was painted primrose and apple green, and is seen here about to embark on the very first service run to Wednesfield. It has just turned round in Princes Square opposite Wulfruna Street and waits in Broad Street outside the Butler's Brewery-owned Vine Hotel; this terminus lasted until 1937 when it was moved into Thornley Street. *O. Wildsmith*

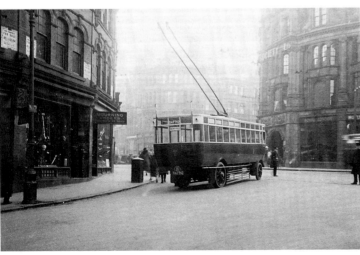

Left Similar trolleybus 2 (DA 7742) is about to turn round at the top of Broad Street by undertaking a U-turn in Princes Square. In front of it is the Royal London Mutual Insurance building, opened in 1902 to the vaguely Dutch designs of Essex, Nicol & Goodman. To the left is a gentlemen's dress hire shop with the appropriate name of 'Mourning Orders'. The terminus of the pioneering 6 route was reached from Cleveland Road depot with the aid of a skate inserted into the track. The long bamboo pole used to retrieve the trolleypoles is stowed along the bottom of the offside of the trolleybus, extending across the rear wheel arch. These early trolleybuses had surprisingly long lives, albeit on pneumatic tyres, the complete batch of 1 to 6 being withdrawn on 24 March 1934. *O. Wildsmith*

Top Wolverhampton's first post-war bus was 384 (FJW 384), a Guy 'Arab' III 6LW with a Brush H29/25R body. There were 15 of these buses in the batch that followed on from the later-numbered Daimler CVG6s, 384 being delivered in November 1948. It is standing in Queen Street working on the 19 service. This had been introduced on 2 June 1947 to serve the new housing estates off the Wednesfield Road trolleybus route using part of the old bus route to the Minerva Inn, Essington, but introducing a new section along Stubby Lane. *A. J. Douglas*

Middle The 60 bus route was jointly worked with Walsall Corporation and followed the line of the 59 trolleybus along Lichfield Road until The Albion public house was reached. It then continued along the A4124 into Bloxwich. Having arrived in Wolverhampton's town centre by way of Piper's Row, the 60 route also started in Queen Street outside the old Dispensary building of 1826. Architecturally the best street in Wolverhampton, Queen Street was something of a backwater as regards its role as a bus terminus for about six bus routes. No 9 (SUK 9) is a rear-entrance MCCW-bodied Guy 'Arab' IV 6LW dating from April 1957, and is loading up ready for the run to Bloxwich. This route was introduced on 9 May 1949, but used protected fares in order to keep 'local' passengers on the existing Wolverhampton Corporation 6 (and later 59) trolleybus service. In later

years the same scheme would also protect the Mossley 31 trolleybus service of Walsall Corporation as it travelled away from Bloxwich along Sneyd Lane. *D. R. Harvey collection*

Bottom Standing in Market Street with its inter-war shops in 1950 is the first 'utility' bus to be delivered to the undertaking. Guy 'Arab' I 358 (DJW 378) has a very early Brush wartime body, of which only 21 were built in this highbridge form on this chassis. No 358 was delivered in November 1942 with a large front destination aperture, which had to be cut down in order to take the smaller Wolverhampton two-line blind. This bus should be displaying the service number 42, which was introduced on 29 July 1949. This went by way of Neachells Lane, crossing the Wednesfield route at The Albion public house at the Stubby Lane junction before going on to the terminus at the Gate Inn, New Invention. Coming along Market Street from the direction of Queen Street is a rather splendid early post-war Humber Super Snipe, while an Austin Big Seven saloon with its swept tail is parked behind the Guy. *A. B. Cross*

Above The inbound trolleybus service from Wednesfield used to climb Broad Street before turning around in Princes Square near Stafford Street, but a new terminus, about 60 yards further away from the town centre, was brought into use on 10 May 1937. On 28 July 1963, having driven up Broad Street, 439 (EJW 439), an early post-war Sunbeam W4 with a 1961 Roe H32/28R body, turns into Thornley Street when working on the 59 route. Parked outside Richmond's furniture store during one of its periodic sales is a slightly battered Austin A35 two-door saloon. All the buildings in this view of 40 years ago have survived to the present day, though many of their uses are less salubrious. *J. C. Brown*

Below Parked in Thornley Street in about 1938 is one of the two Guy 'Arab' 5LW single-deckers with Park Royal B32R bodies that dated from 1935. The problem is, what was it doing here with 20 on the destination blind, as the 20 route went from Bushbury Hill opposite the 3 trolleybus route terminus to Wednesfield, then on to Willenhall? It didn't get anywhere near the town centre, let alone the back of the Territorial Army Drill Hall in Thornley Street! The theory, almost impossible to contradict at this distance of time, is as follows: remembering that the Wednesfield route was worked by single-decker trolleybuses until 1944 because of the low height beneath Broad Street railway bridge, if there was a sudden shortage from the 11 single-deck trolleys that were available in the late 1930s, a single-decker motor bus would have to be substituted. As trolleybuses and motorbuses had their own discrete set of destination blinds, the only destination that a motorbus

going to Wednesfield could display was that for the 20 route. Problem solved – perhaps! *D. R. Harvey collection*

Top The terminus of the 59 route was, for most of its life, in Thornley Street, and it was here that in time-honoured fashion the crew used their turn-round break for a quick 'cough and a drag'. In about 1958, before the take-over by M&B of the Aston-based Atkinson's Brewery the following year, trolleybus 407 (DJW 907) displays an advertisement for the latter's bitter. This trolleybus is a Sunbeam W4 of November 1944 vintage, rebodied by Park Royal in March 1952, and it is working on the 59 route to The Albion Inn on Lichfield Road at Linthouse Lane, which had been extended from Wednesfield on 10 January 1955. *D. R. Harvey collection*

Middle Standing underneath the by now largely unused trolleybus wires in Thornley Street is Park Royal-bodied Guy 'Arab' V 138 (138 DDA), which had entered service in January 1964 in time to replace trolleybuses on the Fordhouses and Bushbury Hill routes. Behind 138 is another Guy 'Arab' V, but with a slightly more angular Weymann body. They are waiting at the back of the Drill Hall at the rather time-expired bus shelters when working on the 59 service. Although the trolleybus route was abandoned on 3 November 1963, the overhead is still in place on 23 July 1964. *D. R. Harvey collection*

Bottom As already mentioned, the low railway bridge in Broad Street meant that until 1943 the Wednesfield route was operated by single-deckers. By this late stage of the Second World War, Wolverhampton had four Sunbeam MF1s of 1934 vintage (206-209), four similarly Park Royal-bodied Guy BTs of the same age (210-213), and three more MF1s (231-233), which were added to the fleet in 1936. The first of these later single-deckers was 231 (JW 8131), which when new had been exhibited at the 1935 Commercial Motor Show at Earls Court. In about 1943, with headlight masks and white blackout paint adorning its wings and 'leading edges', 231 turns out of Whitmore Street and into Westbury Street. The tall building with the steeply pitched slate roof is St Patrick's Roman Catholic Church, a towerless brick building in a Decorated Gothic style designed by E. W. Pugin in 1867 and featuring a large rose window as about its one redeeming feature, which ironically in later years was bricked over with the addition of

a large raised brick crucifix; it was demolished in 1972 to make way for the Ring Road. No 231 was withdrawn on 31 January 1944 together with 211, which had been an accident victim, although five of the MF1s survived until 1949. *D. R. Harvey collection*

Above left Working on the 59 service to The Albion, Wednesfield, on 9 August 1962, Sunbeam W4 trolleybus 437 (EJW 437) travels past the Limerick Inn in Westbury Street, which stood on the corner of Whitmore Street. The vehicle had only re-entered service on 1 February 1962, so the bodybuilder's paintwork still looks nicely reflective with its highly varnished finish. Beyond the car park, on the site of some time-expired tunnel-back houses, is the Warwick Arms, a Butler's-owned public house on the corner of Little's Lane and St Mary's Terrace. Both pubs occupied early Victorian premises that pre-dated the demolished houses, although the Warwick Arms was eventually to succumb to the Ring Road scheme. Behind the Austin Cambridge A55 estate car and the Austin A35 van are the well-advertised rooms of the YMCA Youth Centre. *J. C. Brown*

Below left The turn left from Westbury Street into Broad Street was awkward, being on the quite steep slope of the latter road. Eight-foot-wide Sunbeam F4 460 (FJW 460), which entered service on 4 September 1948 with a Park Royal H28/26R body, makes the turn on 3 November 1962 when working on the 59 service to The Albion Inn on Lichfield Road. This trolleybus was withdrawn on 9 June 1963 when the Penn and Penn Fields routes were closed for trolleybus operation. It was then driven to the back of the perimeter road at Park Lane garage where, with the aid of bamboo poles held by mechanics, it was reversed on to the grass, and there it stood until sold off to Don Everall about two months later for scrap. *W. Ryan*

Above Broad Street fell gently towards the junction with Railway Street and Broad Street bridge over the Birmingham Canal Navigation's Wolverhampton Level. Guy 'Arab' V 141 (141 DDA), one of the 1964 batch of Park Royal-bodied buses, travels towards the canal bridge during 1966 when working on the 59 service,

though the platform staff have not yet turned the destination blind to read 'WEDNESFIELD'. Behind the bus is a three-storey Victorian terrace that disappeared when the Ring Road was cut. Next to the sign reading 'Transport Accommodation' can be seen some of the intricate patterned brickwork on the upper floors, while at ground level is a 'greasy spoon' transport café, frying up delicacies such as black pudding and sausages made by either Marsh & Baxter or Palethorpe. Today this is the site of another car park, alongside St Patrick's Ring Road. *A. D. Broughall*

Below The large post-war Ashmore Park housing estate was squeezed in between the Wednesfield UDC boundary and the north side of Lichfield Road off Linthouse Lane. One of the main routes to serve the estate was the 72 service, which started in the town centre in St James's Square. This headed off down Horseley Fields and into Willenhall, then north towards Wednesfield via Wednesfield Road. It then skirted around the town and crossed Lichfield Road at the trolleybus terminus at the 1950s-built Albion public house before travelling along Linthouse Lane. This bus is 79 (7079 UK), a Guy 'Arab' V with a Weymann H41/31FD body that dated from 1963, and it is just leaving St James's Square on its way to the Ashmore Park Estate. *A. D. Broughall*

Above left While the inbound carriageway of the Broad Street bridge beneath the High Level station was being lowered in the winter of 1943, the 6A trolleybuses initially used the old outward carriageway; all traffic was therefore single line through the bridge, which was operated by stop-go light signals. Once that carriageway was lowered, double-deckers were introduced at once, and 'both-ways' double-decker trolleybus operation commenced on 17 February 1944. Rather battered Park Royal-bodied Sunbeam MF1 209 (JW 4109) comes through the bridge on its way to Wednesfield. With only 32 seats, overloading on this route during wartime single-decker operating conditions was becoming all too regular, and the substitution of double-deckers must have been a relief to everyone, especially the previously squashed passengers. The end of this final route of single-deck operation brought a premature end to six of the 11 trolleybuses, but as they were still only ten years old, odd bits of work were found for the survivors until 1949, when, like their pre-war double-deck counterparts, they were rapidly withdrawn. *J. S. Webb*

Left Emerging from the gloom of the Broad Street railway bridge and about to pass into Wednesfield Road is Roe-rebodied Sunbeam W4 trolleybus 448 (EJW 448). Passing into Wolverhampton is a Ford Consul II 204E, while waiting to come out of the road on the left, which led into the blue-bricked forecourt of Wolverhampton's much missed Low Level station, is one of the ubiquitous Ford Anglia 105Es, of which Dagenham produced an amazing 945,713 examples. The 'BUTLERS BITTER'-bedecked bridge was the last of the low bridges that had affected the use of double-deckers on certain of the trolleybus routes, and upon it to the left is a signal box located beyond the end of the platforms of the High Level station. The trolleybus is passing Lock Street, with a Marsh & Baxter's advertisement on the billboard, while the women waiting at the trolleybus stop are standing at the western end of the railway bridge that passed over the tracks of the former GWR Low Level station. In the far distance, with a Vauxhall Victor F-type passing over it, is Broad Street canal bridge, built in 1879 by Tyldesleys of Willenhall. Next to the Rover car, about to come under the bridge, is the M&B-owned Union Inn. *J. C. Brown*

Above Immediately after the Second World War there were many attempts to build houses that could be assembled 'on site'. The best-known were the 'pre-fabs', but others around the country were built, such as those on the right here, at the corner of Springfield Road. They were known as 'the Cornish flats' and, with their clinker-styled roofs, were a distinctive feature of Wednesfield Road near Inkerman Street. Trolleybus 410 (DJW 940), a wartime Sunbeam W4 rebodied by Park Royal in 1952, when it was only seven years old, travels towards the Chubb lock factory gates on the right on 15 May 1962 on its way towards Heath Town. *J. C. Brown*

Opposite page The first shopping centre away from the town was in Wednesfield Road, Heath Town, seen here looking towards Wolverhampton. On the right, beyond the Edwardian row of shops, which are the only remnant of Heath Town today, is the tall nave end of St Barnabas's Church, completed in 1893 to the designs of T. H. Fleeming, which left the otherwise pleasantly proportioned church without a spire, then immediately before the First World War the open space beyond the church was entirely taken over by the Chubb lock and safe works. Among the turn-of-the-20th-century shops is Martin's boot repair shop, which today is a fish and chip shop. By this time the Lorain contact studs had been replaced by overhead tram wires, a task completed on the Wednesfield 5 tram route on 28 July 1921. Yet 51 weeks later the trams ran to Wednesfield for the last time, and, after an interregnum of three months when motor buses were used, the new 'trolleys' commenced operation to a terminus at Pinfold Bridge, Wednesfield. Thus this scene dates from between 1921 and 1923.

The extent of the late-1960s Heath Town development can be judged when looking out of town along Wednesfield Road today, near where the end of the pedestrian bridge meets Woden Road. This development was designed by A. Chapman in 1963 and completely wiped out the Victorian road layout in Heath Town. On 15 October 2003 two-year-old Travel West Midlands Dennis 'Trident' 4172 (Y772 TOH), with an Alexander H47/28F body, pulls away from the bus stop at the Heath Town Shopping Centre as it travels towards Wolverhampton City Centre along the bus lane. It is about opposite the former St Barnabas's Church seen above, which survives today as a Congregational Church. Behind the blue-painted pedestrian bridge is Campion House, one of several multi-storey residential blocks built in Heath Town at the end of the 1960s. Off the picture to the left is a block of Victorian shops that became the only survivors of the conversion of Wednesfield Road into a dual carriageway. *J. Hughes collection/D. R. Harvey*

Above Wolverhampton Corporation's tram 4 was a single-decker open combination 32-seater built by ER&TCW, mounted on Lorain-DuPont trucks and introduced in May 1902. In later years this body would be rebuilt to become a totally enclosed saloon. Looking towards Wednesfield on a hot sunny day in the summer of 1902, with the shop blinds extended, tram 4 is standing in the passing loop in the centre of Heath Town's shopping centre near where Railway Street, on the left, joined Wednesfield Road. Although this picture was taken more than 100 years ago and everyone on this picture is long dead, people will always be people doing exactly the same things as people today. Several groups of women stop for a natter. Folks have come out to have a look at the photographer, because people are always curious. The curse of urbanisation before the arrival of the motor car was horse manure, and there is enough in Wednesfield Road to help with the rhubarb crop! What is missing in these infant days of horseless motive power are motor cars, as well as the usual electrical overhead equipment for the trams. Between the rails are the surface contact studs of the Lorain system. The building with the porticoed entrance on the corner of Railway Street is Lloyds Bank, which had opened only a few years earlier. Railway Street led to the Culwell engineering and cycle manufacturing works and to the LNWR's Heath Town goods station. On the corner of Cross Street, on the right, is the Butler's Brewery-owned Star Hotel, which, like all the properties here, would be swept away in the mid-1960s. Just visible above the terraced shops on the right is the weather-vaned spire of the Wesleyan Chapel, built in 1856, while incongruously on the nearer corner of Dean Street is the New Inn public house. *J. Hughes collection*

Left Heath Town was already under threat of redevelopment well before the closure of the Wednesfield trolleybus route, as shown here by the demolition of the properties on the left of Wednesfield Road at the corner of Grove Street. The Congregational Chapel on the corner of distant Frederick Street, with its little cupola, was built in 1886, but would be lost in the Heath Town redevelopment of the next few years. In fact, the houses on the corner of Railway Street, opposite the distant Lloyds Bank building, appear to be partly derelict already. On 15 March 1962 440 (EJW 440), a 1947 Sunbeam W4 chassis rebodied by Roe in February 1961, passes the peculiarly towered building on the corner of Paul Street. The nearer three-storey buildings, including those occupied by the greengrocer, W. Jacques, date from approximately the 1850s, 20 or so years older than the grocer's and chemist's shops that the trolleybus is passing. The nearest parked car is a very early Ford Consul EOTA, registered in Wolverhampton in 1951. In the shadow of the trolleybus is an Austin A40 Somerset, while behind the Thornycroft Nippy van is an early post-war Austin 16. *J. C. Brown*

Below left The children on the far-off swings will be oblivious to Roe-rebodied Sunbeam W4 trolleybus 452 (EJW 452) as it passes Heath Town Park on 9 August 1962 on its way to Wednesfield. The park was opened in 1920 on three plots of land that stretched from opposite Holy Trinity Church in Church Street through to the main Wolverhampton Road, utilising in part a large tract of land reclaimed from the clay workings of a brickworks. Over the raised bank on the left is the BCN's Wyrley & Essington Canal of 1797, while just around the distant bend is Church Street and the tunnel beneath the Wolverhampton Road that carries the former Grand Junction Railway line through Heath Town. *J. C. Brown*

Top right Overtaking an Austin A40 Dorset two-door saloon is Sunbeam F4 467 (FJW 467), which entered service with its 8-foot-wide Park Royal H28/26R body on 2 October 1948. Coming down the hill in Wolverhampton Road, it has just passed the New Cross Hospital entrance, where the young girls are walking; today's modern New Cross Hospital serves the whole of Wolverhampton in 'state-of-the-art' medical premises, but it originated as the Wolverhampton Workhouse, opened in 1903 to the designs of A. Marshall, some three years after building work had begun. It became a hospital during the 1920s and today has in excess of 2,500 beds. Behind the 19th-century houses on the right is the Wyrley & Essington Canal. *J. C. Brown*

Above Also seen at New Cross Hospital, Wolverhampton Road, but on the first day of the new Wednesfield trolleybus service, 29 October 1923, trolleybus 2 (DA 7742), a Dodson-bodied Tilling-Stevens TS6, squeezes past the almost predatory Albion 25hp tower wagon, parked almost malevolently awaiting de-wirements or worse! When new in 1914, this tower wagon had been motorbus 3, with a Roberts B24F body, but in 1920 it was converted into this service vehicle. Despite appearances, the trolleybus is going back to Wolverhampton, having successfully introduced 'trackless' trolleys to the town. In these early pioneering days the overhead for the trolleybuses was spaced at a rather narrow 12 inches, but after 1930 it was widened to the more usual 18 inches. Initially single-deckers had been introduced so that the low railway bridges in the town, including that in Broad Street, could be negotiated; little was it realised that it would be more than 20 years before double-deckers would work on the Wednesfield service. *D. R. Harvey collection*

Above By the 1960s the rapidly expanding New Cross Hospital was being served directly into the grounds by the Corporation. One such route was the 76, which went from the town centre at Exchange Street to the hospital. Daimler CVG6 515 (FJW 515), which entered service in February 1950 with a Brush body, threads its way out of the hospital grounds, leaving behind a lot of building development, scaffolding and a large mobile crane. It is Saturday 13 December 1969, and the elderly Daimler, still in Wolverhampton livery, passes groups of people who have completed their visits to patients in the hospital wards. *M. R. Keeley*

Below left Standing at the New Street terminus in Wolverhampton Road just short of Rookery Bridge is car 4. This tram had entered service in May 1902 as one of the cars that opened the system. It was built by G. F. Milnes as an open combination single-decker, but the eight seats at either end of the car, four seats on either side of the bulkheads, proved unsatisfactory, and as early as 1903 car 4 was converted to a 32-seater saloon tramcar. The Wednesfield Road tram service had been opened initially as far as Church Street on 22 June 1904 and was extended on 31 October 1904, when the crowds on the corner of New Street, by the lamp standard, came out to greet the arrival of car 4. To celebrate the event, the house at the terminus was given the name plaque Lorain Villa. The tram route had been authorised under the Wolverhampton Corporation Act of 1904 as Route 1, but the extension over Rookery Bridge into High Street, Wednesfield, as Route 2, was never constructed as its operation was dependent upon the widening and reconstruction of the latter bridge over the meandering Wyrley & Essington Canal, which did not take place during the lifetime of tramcar operation along Wednesfield Road. *Commercial postcard*

Above Before the official opening of Wolverhampton's first trolleybus route to Wednesfield on 29 October 1923, certain trials were made to test the equipment and the first batch of vehicles. Trolleybuses were in their infancy, and still being referred to as 'tracklesses', when, after being impressed with the recently opened Nechells route in Birmingham, the General Manager, Charles Owen Silvers, that doyen of the trolleybus 'movement', recommended that the worn-out tram tracks to Wednesfield be replaced by trolleybuses. While Wolverhampton was not among the pioneers of trolleybuses, its historical position of being only the 15th system to open in the UK definitely puts it into the second tranche of trolleybus operators, which included near neighbour Birmingham, Ashton-under Lyne, Ipswich, Nottingham and Southend-on-Sea. Of those 15 early operators that followed Bradford's lead in June 1911, five closed very quickly and at least three other 'systems' closed without leaving any lasting impression. Without any Parliamentary Powers to operate trolley vehicles, retrospective permission was given by the Ministry of Transport for the Wednesfield service to open, which extended the former 1¾-mile tram route to 2¼ miles, over the by now rebuilt Rookery Bridge and into Wednesfield's town centre. By 1929 the Wolverhampton trolleybus system was the largest in the world, with a fleet of 61 vehicles and 25 route miles; unfortunately, five years later the system was virtually completed and the excitement was over. That, however, was in the future as trolleybus 1 (DA 7741), a Tilling-Stevens TS6 with a Dodson B40C body, stands opposite Lorain Villa at the old tram terminus in Wednesfield Road and alongside the workshop of John Griffiths, an iron merchant whose building had the distinction of having a GPO post-box set into its wall. The Inspector looks sternly at the photographer as he stands on the corner of New Street, but just look at that smug expression on the front of the trolleybus, having crossed Rookery Bridge, which the trams were unable to do! Trolleybuses 1, Trams lost! *O. Wildsmith*

Above Travelling away from the centre of Wednesfield's, along Rookery Street, on 30 August 1962, is 448 (EJW 448), one of the Roe-rebodied Sunbeam W4s, working on the 59 route back into Wolverhampton. This section of road was authorised for tramcar operation but was never implemented due to the unsuitability of the bridge for tram track. The trolleybus is approaching Rookery Bridge where the tram terminus was located, while just visible on the left in Wednesfield's High Street is the Wesleyan Chapel. Hall Street led to a lock on the Wyrley & Essington Canal and also gave access by the 'back door' to Wednesfield railway station, opened on 1 November 1872, on the Walsall to Wolverhampton line. *J. C. Brown*

Below left In High Street, Wednesfield, trolleybus 410 (DJW 940), a 1945 Sunbeam W4 chassis with a 1952 Park Royal body, pulls away from the tree-lined churchyard of the town's Parish Church, with its destination box already turned for its return journey. St Thomas's Church was built in 1751 and, having been enlarged twice during the Victorian period, was all but burned to the ground on 18 January 1902. It was subsequently rebuilt during the following year at a cost of £5,000 to a larger plan designed by local architect F. T. Beck. Facing Wolverhampton outside the interwar block of shops with its own service road, is one of the town's 99 8-foot-wide Park Royal trolleybuses, and towering, towerless, above it is Wednesfield's Wesleyan Chapel. It was here at the Dog & Partridge public house, one of the oldest buildings in Wednesfield, which stood alongside

Pinfold Bridge, that the trolleybuses terminated on the opening day of the route on 29 October 1923. *C. Carter*

Top On that opening day, 29 October 1923, Driver Eccleston is in the cab and Inspector Jeavons stands in front of Wolverhampton's first trolleybus, wearing looks of military bearing and justifiable pride in this great municipal achievement. Wolverhampton's trolleybus system was opened only seven weeks after that in Ipswich, which also was initially a devotee of single-deckers. Tilling-Stevens TS6 1 (DA 7741) has a centre-entrance Dodson body that looks as if one had to be fairly fit in order to climb into the spartanly seated saloon. The bus is at the original Wednesfield terminus of the 6 route at the turning circle at Neachells Lane, near the Dog & Partridge public house. In the left background can be seen the brick parapet of Pinfold Bridge over the Wyrley & Essington Canal. *J. Hughes collection*

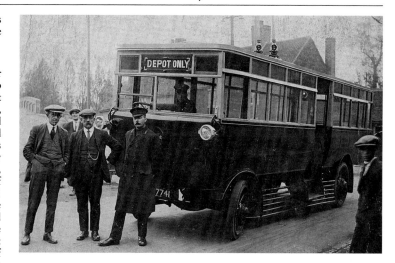

Middle The first genuine post-war trolleybuses to be purchased were 26 Sunbeam F4s with Park Royal H28/26R 8-foot-wide bodies; 470 (FJW 470) entered service on 23 October 1948 and survived until 9 June 1963, when it was made redundant after the closure of the trolleybus services to Penn Fields and Penn. It is about to cross Pinfold Bridge over the Wyrley & Essington Canal, where the trolleybuses turned into Neachells Lane to terminate until the route was extended to Wood End Road on 10 February 1934. The Ford Thames Trader lorry, a model that was designed in Germany, turns into Neachells Lane in front of the old cottages. *D. R. Harvey collection*

Bottom On 10 August 1962 Roe-rebodied Sunbeam W4 435 (EJW 435) has negotiated Pinfold Bridge and travels along Lichfield Road, having re-entered service with its new body only eight months earlier on 1 January 1962. It is travelling up the slight rise past Duke Street on the left and the very mixed-age housing in this section of Lichfield Road, as it goes towards the second terminus at Wood End Road, bound for the 59 route's outer terminus at The Albion public house. Just beyond the approaching trolleybus, set back on the left, is the Vine hostelry, and beyond that a terrace of 1930s-built shops with their own private service road. *J. C. Brown*

Below The second trolleybus terminus on the Wednesfield route was at Wood End. The service was not completely converted to double-deck operation until 17 February 1944, so single-decker operation on the 6A route remained for most of the Second World War. Fitted with headlight masks and white-painted body edgings, 213 (JW 4313), a Guy BT with a quite pretty Park Royal B32R body, stands at the inbound loading stop in Lichfield Road having negotiated the turning loop across the continuation of that road, which is to the rear of the trolleybus. No 213 entered service on 1 November 1934, but was one of the six single-deckers quickly taken out of service once the railway bridge in Broad Street had been lowered, in the case of 213 on the last day of January 1945. *D. R. Harvey collection*

Bottom Waiting just beyond the Wood End Road junction in Lichfield Road beneath the trolleybus wires at the terminus of the 6 route is Daimler COG5 344 (BJW 144) of 1938, a

somewhat care-worn Brush-bodied 54-seater, on its way to Willenhall in about 1954 when working on the 20 service. The bus had started on this inter-suburban service from Bushbury Hill and would travel along the High Street before heading along Waddens Brook Lane towards Willenhall. Despite the sagging waistrail of the body, 344 would remain in service until late 1957. (The other end of the 20 route is described in the Park Lane to Bushbury Hill section.) *R. Hannay*

Right By 30 August 1962 the Wood End Road island was serving as a turn-back point for the 6 route shortworking, and 402 (DJW 902), the first of the wartime Sunbeam W4 trolleybuses to be rebodied by Park Royal, has travelled from The Albion terminus by way of Lichfield Road, which is behind the trolleybus. This section of the Wednesfield route along the A4124 was opened on 10 January 1955, making it the penultimate trolleybus route extension in Wolverhampton. The final extension of the 9 route to the Pheasant public house at the junction of Lower Prestwood Road and Wood End Lane opened some 18 months later. The next extension, along Linthouse Lane, again serving a new area of housing, was never constructed; following a meeting of the Transport Committee in June 1957, the first inclinations that the trolleybuses would be abandoned surfaced. This was a great pity, as the extension would have linked the terminus of the 9 route with that of the 59, making another valuable circular service. *J. C. Brown*

Below right Trolleybus 460 (FJW 460), a Sunbeam F4 with a Park Royal body that had entered service on 4 September 1948, is in Lichfield Road travelling out of town. The road on the right with the tall poplar trees hiding the inter-war semi-detached houses is Hyde Road. It is 10 August 1962 and to the left of the trolleybus, behind the padlocked gates, are the single-storey barrel-roof classrooms of Wards Bridge Secondary School, named after the crossing of the Wyrley & Essington Canal next to the inter-war houses on the distant skyline. This was the third and final bridge over this section of the Birmingham Canal Navigation that was crossed by the 59 trolleybus service. The building framing the approaching trolleybus is the sloping roof and glass frontage of what was then the school's main hall and which today is part of the Jenny Lee Centre. On the left, coming out of Lakefield Road, which today is the main by-pass road around Wednesfield, is a Seddon Mark 7 municipally owned lorry. *J. C. Brown*

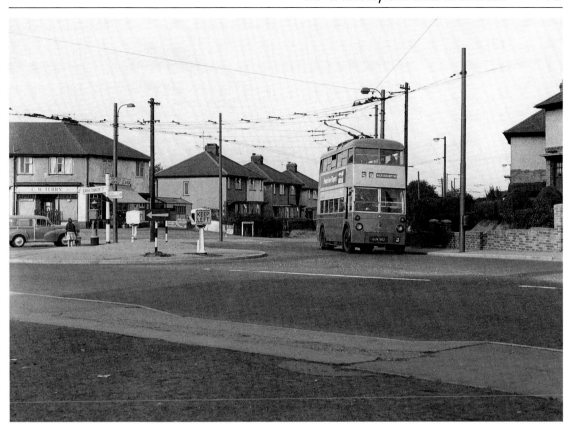

Above One of the 8-foot-wide Park Royal-bodied Sunbeam F4s, 472 (FJW 472), dating from 1948, is working into Wednesfield town centre from The Albion terminus on the 59 route on 2 October 1963, just a month before it was withdrawn together with the Wednesfield trolleybus route. It is in Lichfield Road at Lyndale Drive, and is passing the site of Wednesfield High School. The three-storey maisonettes beyond the service road on the left date from the 1950s, while parked in front of them is a Birmingham-registered Ford Popular 103G. Following the trolleybus are a Ford Thames Trader and a Morris-Commercial Series III lorry. *J. C. Brown*

Left On 13 July 1962 trolleybus 451 (EJW 451), a 1948 Sunbeam W4 rebodied by Roe in the spring of 1961, enters the turning loop in Lichfield Road opposite The Albion public house at Linthouse Lane. The municipal-owned housing had its own service road, and parked just before the trolleybus turning circle is a Ford Prefect E493A four-door saloon. As the two RAF servicemen wait at the corner of Linthouse Lane, the trolleybus will turn round and head back to the town centre. It would not use the bus stop on the left as this was reserved for the 60 bus route to Bloxwich that was jointly worked with Walsall Corporation. *J. C. Brown*

Top Standing in the turning loop at the Wednesfield terminus of the 59 route is trolleybus 471 (FJW 471). It is 19 May 1963 and the vehicle is waiting in the lay-by opposite The Albion public house. This Park Royal-bodied Sunbeam F4 of 1948 was one of six trolleybuses to be repainted in the experimental dark green livery between December 1959 and July 1963. It was the last of the six to be repainted into fleet livery, and survived until 25 November 1964. As far back as the early 1950s it had been realised that the Wednesfield service was inadequate, terminating at Wood End Road as the 6 route, so on 1 March 1954 a new motorbus service numbered 59 was introduced, extending the route to The Albion public house on the corner of Stubby Lane and Lichfield Road opposite the turning loop adjacent to Linthouse Lane. This service was replaced by trolleybuses on 10 January 1955. *W. Ryan*

Middle Travelling along Sneyd Lane on its way to Wolverhampton when working on the 60 service is 579 (KJW 579), which has just crossed the railway line near Bloxwich station on the old South Staffordshire line between Walsall and Cannock, which closed under Dr Beeching's abandonments of 1963. The old station was subsequently demolished, but after much campaigning Centro re-opened the line in 1989, and with it a new station halt was built adjacent to the old Bloxwich station. For many years the land next to the railway line to the left of the bridge was occupied by a small estate of 'pre-fabs'. Trolleybus 579 was one of the batch of seven Guy 'Arab' IVs with Gardner 6LW engines and Metro-Cammell 'Orion' H31/25R bodies that had entered service in June 1954. Unusually for this body style, they incorporated Birmingham-style straight staircases. The bus is operating beneath the Walsall Corporation trolleybus wires of the 31 route to the Mossley Estate, a route opened by the Corporation on 3 June 1957. *R. F. Mack*

Bottom The terminus of the 60 route in Bloxwich was in High Street, near the Bulls Head public house of 1938, with its distinctive mock-Tudor frontage; the buses used Park Road, on the right, as a turning circle. To the left of the bus, underneath the trees, is the bus shelter and toilets, while behind the distant BMMO pre-war SOS FEDD and Walsall Corporation wartime Guy 'Arab' II are ornamental gardens and the ornate fountains that were to become a distinctive feature of Bloxwich in the post-war years. The bus, advertising the Wolverhampton-based Beatties department store, is 506 (FJW 506), a Daimler CVG6 with a Brush H29/25R body that had entered service in 1948, just a year before the 60 route was introduced. *J. S. Webb*

To Great Bridge and West Bromwich

A bus route that represented quite a late arrival was the service between Wolverhampton and West Bromwich. This was the 90 route, introduced on 17 October 1948 and operated as a joint service by Wolverhampton and West Bromwich Corporations. At first the service carried minimum fares outwards from Wolverhampton and from West Bromwich in order to discourage short-distant passengers. Because of objections from Midland Red, which operated by way of the New Road (A4123), the route went via Bilston, Moxley, Wednesbury and Hill Top. This partly mirrored the old South Staffordshire Tramway's 'Black Country Through Service' between Birmingham, West Bromwich and Darlaston, which had been implemented on 9 October 1912. The 90 bus service followed the Holyhead Road route at Moxley rather than travelling via Darlaston's Bull Stake and on to the White Horse at Wednesbury. Wolverhampton was keen to replicate the old tram route by running into Birmingham, but this had to wait until after the formation of the West Midlands PTE and the introduction of its 79 bus service.

The Wolverhampton town terminus was originally intended to be in Bilston Street, but this was deemed too narrow and the less convenient St George's Parade, just outside St George's Churchyard and near Cleveland Road garage, was used instead. The route went out of town by way of Bilston Road beneath the trolleybus wires of the 2 and 7 services, before travelling on via Moxley and Wednesbury to the West Bromwich terminus in Queen Street.

Below The 90 route to West Bromwich began on 17 October 1948, despite originally being proposed more than 30 months earlier. Cross-boundary bus services were comparatively rare in the post-war years and the proposed integrated West Bromwich-Wolverhampton joint service was objected to by the hostile Midland Red company. This led to the delay in the introduction of the new 90 route. The original terminus was in St George's Parade alongside the delightful St George's Church; this Commissioners' church, designed by James Morgan in a Classical style with a portal and Tuscan columns, was consecrated in 1830 and closed in 1978. It was imaginatively saved by Sainsburys in 1987, which incorporated it into its supermarket development. In the 1960s the terminus was transferred to outside the Wulfrun Shopping Centre in Cleveland Street. Standing empty outside the churchyard with its front wheel scotched is 528 (FJW 528), a Daimler CVG6 with a Brush H29/25R body, dating from March 1950; one wonders just how many people realise that Sainsburys car park was a Victorian mass grave for the town's cholera victims in 1849! *W. J. Haynes*

Above right The wires are still just about up, but the power has been switched off and the trolleybuses, with their unique 'electric' smell, have recently departed for the last time. Passing Cleveland Road depot, but from this day onwards a garage, on Monday 6 March 1967, is Guy 'Arab' IV 17 (SUK 17), working on the 90 service to West Bromwich. This Metro-Cammell 'Orion'-bodied bus was unusual on several counts: its lightweight body was equipped with a straight staircase, which was an added expense as the rest of the body specification was pared down to the minimum. It also had the Meadows 10.45-litre 6DC engine, built locally at the factory in Park Lane.

Wolverhampton Corporation had a total of 14 of these extremely powerful diesel engines, of which 12 were fitted into buses in the SUK 1-18 batch. This brief dalliance at supporting local industry was soon regretted as the Meadows engines were comparatively fragile and needed a lot more 'TLC' than a Gardner 6LW engine. Behind the bus, on the corner of Vicarage Road, is a factory built originally to house a boot and shoe manufacturer. *J. Hughes collection*

Below Long before the 90 motorbus route was even a twinkle in Mr Silvers's mind, Cleveland Road depot had been the home of trolleybus operation in the town. The original electric tramcar shed was opened in 1901 opposite the Wolverhampton & Staffordshire Infirmary in readiness for the first Lorain Surface Contact stud route, which opened along Bilston Road on 6 February 1902, while the main offices followed suit that very same year, transferring from the old horse tram depot in Darlington Street. Extensions to the tram depot were made in 1904, 1909, 1913 and 1921, each taking the depot's buildings over the site of the old open-air cattle market as far as Transport Road. Buses were first operated from here in September 1905, while trolleybuses first *reversed* out of the depot into Cleveland

Road on 29 October 1923, as every trolleybus would do until the final closure in 1967. A final expansion on the last plot in Cleveland Road occurred in 1932, just one year after Bilston Street garage was opened. Under the 'MUNICIPAL TRAMWAYS CAR DEPOT' sign, a group of six early double-decker trolleybuses are posed in Cleveland Road. They are displaying route numbers 1, 4 and 7A, suggesting that this picture was set up after May 1929, when the Darlaston trolleybus route was opened. Although ungainly looking by today's standards, in 1929, when Wolverhampton's trolleybus system was briefly the largest in the world, these Dodson-bodied Guy BTX double-deckers were about as modern as one could get! From the right they are 58 (UK 6358), which entered service on 4 May 1929, then 40 (UK 640), of September 1927, one of the first seven trolleybuses in Wolverhampton to have their staircases enclosed. The third vehicle, masked by a group of drivers, conductors and inspectors, is another of the 34-40 batch of Guy BTXs. On the left are 59 (UK 6359), available for service on the day before the opening of the Darlaston trolleybus service and later used as a demonstrator for Nottingham City Transport, 41 (UK 3941), and 55 (UK 5955). *O. Wildsmith*

Below Temporarily driverless, 125 (125 DDA), a Guy 'Arab' V with a Park Royal H41/31F body that entered service in December 1963, stands opposite Cleveland Road garage in 1968 – it looks as if has been abandoned alongside the kerb, rather than parked! On the left and next door to the garage is the three-storey early Victorian Newmarket Hotel, while the tall building at the end of Cleveland Road is the premises of Dixons, the wallpaper and paint retailer. The terminus of the 90 route by this time had been moved to Cleveland Street, so inbound crews were more likely to change outside the garage than at the town terminus. *D. J. Little*

Bottom The 90 route left Wolverhampton by way of Cleveland Road and Bilston Road on its way to Bilston and Wednesbury. The large Wolverhampton & Staffordshire General Hospital stands to the left of the distant Cleveland Road; officially opened on 1 January 1849, it was extended many times before being renamed the Royal Hospital in 1923, and would survive into NHS days, not finally closing

until the enormous expansion of the New Cross Hospital in the late 1980s. Towering above the bus is the premises of Dixons, the long established home decoration retailer. Turning out of Cleveland Road into Bilston Road in 1967 when working on the 90 service is one of the awful Strachan-bodied Guy 'Arab' Vs, 155 (DDA 155C). This bus entered service in February 1965 with this poor quality Metro-Cammell look-alike body, and would be withdrawn after its first Certificate of Fitness was due in 1972, becoming one of the first of the batch of ten to go. On the right is the Cleveland Court Club, formerly a police station, but under the ownership of one Dougie Eades it became the first night club in Wolverhampton. *A. J. Douglas*

Opposite top On leaving Wednesbury, the 90 route followed the route of the old South Staffordshire Tramways tram service by way of Hill Top, before reaching Carter's Green, then continuing along High Street into West Bromwich. On the 90 service is Wolverhampton Corporation's 581. Registered KJW 581 in June 1954, this Metro-Cammell-bodied 56-seater makes an interesting comparison with West Bromwich Corporation's 184 (KEA 184) behind it, which had a similar MCCW 'Orion' body; it is a Daimler CVG6 dating from March 1955, working on the 74 service from Dudley to Birmingham. Coming out of Carter's Green, the buses are passing Shaftesbury Street where for many years Frank Guest's car showrooms were located. On the right, Guest's second-hand car lot is selling a Triumph Renown and an Austin 10hp. *D. R. Harvey collection*

Opposite middle The West Bromwich Building Society and West Bromwich Albion FC were two of the town's nationally best-known products. The

90 service worked into West Bromwich by way of High Street, and here bus 583 (KJW 583), a Guy 'Arab' IV with a Metro-Cammell 'Orion' H30/26R body, is leaving the town past the Building Society's premises travelling towards Carter's Green. Following is West Bromwich Corporation's 139 (CEA 739), a Daimler CVD6 with another MCCW-built body working on the 29 Circular clockwise route, which would follow the green and yellow interloper as far as Hill Top, before turning off to Hateley Heath and All Saints. *D. R. Harvey collection*

Below The West Bromwich terminus of the 90 route was in Queen Street, about 250 yards west of Dartmouth Square and somewhat out of the way when compared with many of the other routes that West Bromwich Corporation jointly operated. Wolverhampton's 531 (FJW 531), a Daimler CVG6 with a Brush H29/25R body, stands alongside the advertising hoarding in Queen Street in about 1961, as an almost new Austin Seven Mini pulls out to overtake the parked bus. Alongside the bus is an advertisement for the long-forgotten Stardrops cleaner, which for 1s 3d appeared to be able to wash everything from dishes to the car. On leaving the terminus the 90 route literally just went around the block, turning left into Pitt Street and left again into New Street before turning right into High Street again. *D. R. Harvey collection*

Whitmore Reans, Bilston and Darlaston

The Corporation's first electric tram route had been between Cleveland Road and Ettingshall Road. This opened on 6 February 1902 using the Lorain Stud Collection system and was extended as far as Stow Heath Lane on 24 September 1902 to meet the Company service from Bilston, which of course was on the overhead system. The Wolverhampton District Electric Tramways finally opened the route between Stow Heath Lane via Bilston, Moxley and Darlaston in 1902, operating over South Staffordshire's tracks. Additionally, there was a short route operated by the Company between Bilston and Bradley via Loxdale Street, which in turn would be taken over by the Corporation. By late 1902 the cross-town tram service to Coleman Street, Whitmore Reans, had been established, extended to Hunter Street on 26 January 1905. During that year negotiations between the Company and the Corporation eventually allowed dual-equipped tramcars to run through to Bilston Town Hall from 9 November.

The Bilston Road 7 tram route was the second service on the system to be converted to overhead operation on 15 June 1921, while the Bilston to Stow Heath Lane section was taken over on 27 August 1928 when the Wolverhampton to Bilston route closed, ending genuine Corporation tramcar routes in the town. The Bradley route and the Bilston to Darlaston service continued to be operated by trams after the Corporation had taken over the Wolverhampton District Electric Tramways services on 1 September 1928, finally ending on 30 November of that year.

The Whitmore Reans electric tram section, by now numbered 2, had been converted to overhead collection on 28 August 1921, but the trams stopped running on 1 October 1927 and were replaced by Guy CX motorbuses until they in turn were replaced by trolleybuses on 27 January 1930. (The route description can be found in Part 2.)

The trolleybus route to Bilston was opened on 19 November 1928, and extended to Darlaston on 25 May 1929, when Dodson-bodied Guy BTX 60 (UK 6360) ceremonially opened the route from the Bull Stake, specially displaying the number 1 in the destination box. The Whitmore Reans route was the next trolleybus route to open in Wolverhampton, on 27 January 1930, and was linked with the Darlaston route at the same time. There was a branch into the Courtauld's factory complex off Hordern Road, but this was closed in late October 1949. Confusingly, the service was numbered 2 and 7, but this was not 2 in one direction across town and 7 in the other; in fact, the 2 went around the Courtauld's loop via Court Road in a clockwise direction, and the 7 went anti-clockwise from Hordern Road into Court Road, with its turn-of-the-20th century housing. In 1940 there was a proposal to convert the wartime motorbus services to Pendeford into trolleybus services utilising unused traction poles from Bournemouth, but this interesting idea, comparable to the Rover extension along Lode Lane in Solihull by Birmingham Corporation, was never sanctioned. After this, the important cross-town trolleybus service from Whitmore Reans to Darlaston continued unaltered until it was abandoned on 8 August 1965.

The motorbus services that went beyond the trolleybus terminus in Whitmore Reans included the 14 to Windermere Road; this alternated across the town to Thompson Avenue with the Blakeley Green 34 route, which during the Second World War served the Boulton Paul aircraft factory at Pendeford. The 63 service, introduced on 27 February 1950 to serve new housing developments, went to Wobaston Road, Bilbrook, and the 15 went into Codsall, to the Crown public house, a service that began on 17 November 1923 when it was taken over from the Great Western Railway.

On the other side of the town centre, the

trolleybuses passed Bilston Street bus garage before turning into Bilston Road, which, unlike today, lined with car showrooms, was a road containing factories, coal yards and, after the Second World War, the many businesses of the motor entrepreneur, Don Everall. Having gone beneath the former LNWR railway line and the first real area of terraced suburban Victorian housing, the trolleybuses and the 90 bus route to West Bromwich forked left at Ettingshall Road towards Wellington Road. As Bilston was neared so the 19th-century houses changed from terraces to semi-detached and finally, within site of Mount Pleasant, large attractive Regency villas became dominant. Along Lichfield Street as far as Bilston's Town Hall the road was shared with the 25 trolleybus route between Fighting Cocks and Willenhall.

The first shortworking point was here in Oxford Street, where trolleybuses only going to Bilston reversed back into Frazer Street, a manoeuvre that was, for the trolleybus crews at least, mercifully not repeated (except for depot workings) after 29 October 1949, when the 47 was extended almost to Moxley, where it turned back in a loop erected in Great Bridge Road. About half a mile earlier, back towards Bilston, the 23 and 24 motorbus services turned into Loxdale Street before travelling the short distance into Bradley, mirroring the former WDET tram service.

From Great Bridge Road, where several large inter-war factory complexes had been built, through Moxley to Darlaston was but a short journey along roads lined with unappealing Victorian houses of various ages, quality and size, before the shops that led to the Bull Stake began to supersede the residential properties.

The 89 route went from Victoria Square to Albrighton and Cosford by way of Wergs Road, which also doubled as the main A41 Holyhead Road. The routes to the north-west of Wolverhampton used this route and the Codsall Road to reach the villages beyond the County Borough Boundary. Although 512 (FJW 512), a Daimler CVG6 with a Brush H29/25R body that entered service in October 1948, looks at first sight as if it is travelling along a country road, it is passing the officers' married quarters – houses to the non-military like you and me – at RAF Cosford when travelling along the tree-lined Sydnal Lane on the 89 service back into Wolverhampton in about 1968. To the left was the important RAF hospital, which served as the major military medical centre for the West Midlands Group. On the opposite side of the A41, near the railway station, is the location of the splendid Aerospace Museum, which also housed for many years the indoor Amateur Athletics Association's Championships. *A. B. Cross*

Top The first batch of six-wheeled Guy CX motorbuses to be equipped with roller number destination boxes on their Dodson H30/25R bodies was numbered 51-54, and delivered in 1927, being also some of the first double-deckers to be fitted with an enclosed staircase in the Corporation fleet. This example has travelled by way of Whitmore Reans and Claregate, and is standing, with its crew posing in front of this normal-control vehicle, next to the Bull Hotel in the Square in Codsall, having worked into the village on the 14 route in about 1933. At this time the Bull was advertising itself as having 'good motor accommodation, pleasure grounds, a bowling green and the facilities to cater for parties'. *Commercial postcard*

Middle Codsall village, with its Victorian-built parish church with Norman remnants and its own railway station, lies about 4 miles from Wolverhampton, but for many years had been losing the battle against the constantly advancing suburban creep of Wolverhampton. At the western end of Codsall village, bus 9 (SUK 9), a Guy 'Arab' IV that entered service in April 1957 with a Metro-Cammell H33/27R body, is standing at the Moat Brook Avenue terminus when working on the 15 service in about 1959. Beyond the bus is an Austin 10/4 dating from about 1936. The bus conductor stands alongside the half-cab bonnet and talks to his driver through the open cabside window, attracting the attention of a young boy and girl. Having reversed into Moat Brook Avenue from Wood Road, the bus will return across town via Claregate to Thompson Avenue. It is carrying an advertisement for OMO washing powder, introduced in 1954, just a year after its arch washing-day rival, Daz. *J. Hughes*

Bottom One of the two ill-fated Guy Motors 'Wulfrunian' FDWs delivered to the undertaking, 70 (4070 JW), fitted with an East Lancs H42/30F body, travels along Codsall Road, Claregate, on the 63 route coming from Bilbrook with its destination blind not changed for the return journey. The bus, the 15th 'Wulfrunian' to be constructed, was delivered in December 1961 and, unlike the Corporation's second uniquely styled 'Wulfrunian', was built with the usual front entrance, air suspension, disc brakes and a nearside-mounted rear ascending staircase. It is passing the recreation ground, with children playing on the distant swings and roundabout, while behind it is the distant 1930s-styled petrol station in the crook of Codsall Road and Pendeford Avenue. The bus is being followed by a Ford Consul 204E convertible, registered in Rochdale in the summer of 1960. The Lane Green area in Bilbrook had been developed in the 1930s at a time when the demand for re-armament to counter the German military threat meant that manufacturers of materiel were swinging into full production. One such was Boulton Paul at Fordhouses, which was involved in the housing development at Pendeford to accommodate its rapidly burgeoning workforce. Although during the Second World War the Corporation ran many Works Services, but it was not until 27 February 1950 that Bilbrook was regularly served when the 63 route was introduced. *R. F. Mack*

Above right The 34 cross-town service to Thompson Avenue from The Pilot public house at Blakeley Green travelled along Hordern Road towards Whitmore Reans. Within a short distance, Guy 'Arab' IV 24 (YDA 24), with an MCCW full-fronted 72-seater body, will reach the trolleybus wires of the 2 and 7 route at the junction with Court Road, and is climbing up the hill from the distant Smestow Valley past the railings protecting the huge Courtauld's factory. For a time, after its Radford Works in Coventry had been destroyed, Daimler resumed production of its bus chassis in the Courtauld's factory complex during December 1942. This resulted in virtually all wartime bus and trolleybus chassis, by Guy, Daimler and the Sunbeam/Karrier badge-engineered W4 examples, being manufactured in Wolverhampton. *A. B. Cross*

Below Trolleybus 624 (FJW 624), a Sunbeam F4 with a Park

Royal H28/26R body, stands at the terminus in Court Road, Whitmore Reans, about to turn into Hordern Road with one of the four Courtauld's Dunstall Works chimneys towering above the late-Victorian houses. The American-owned Courtauld's company set up its factory in 1916, though it was not operational until 1924. It produced viscose yarn, and by the mid-1930s was employing 3,600 workers. So important was the works that the company paid £450 for the installation of wiring into it by way of the main service road, which terminated in a turning circle. This opened on the same day as the new Whitmore Reans trolleybus service, but was discontinued in the autumn of 1949. The last of the bay-windowed terraced housing in Court Road was called Craigstone Villas, built in 1910, and parked outside, facing Hordern Road, is a two-tone Ford Consul 204E Mark II saloon, first registered in Portsmouth in 1958. The car is being washed by its owner, who will probably get a better result than the possessor of the line of washing that has been neatly hung out to dry in the shadow of a grimy conveyor belt in the adjacent factory grounds. *R. F. Mack*

Below The only difference between the 2 and 7 routes was at Whitmore Reans. The theory was that once they got into the Court Road loop at the Courtauld's factory, the 2 service went round clockwise and the 7 anti-clockwise. A man holds on to his bicycle as trolleybus 480 (FJW 480), a Sunbeam F4 with a Park Royal H28/26R body dating from October 1948, turns from Hordern Road into Court Road. It is passing the Butler's-owned Golden Eagle public house on the corner, which dated from 1928 and at the time of writing has been recently renovated. Courtauld's chimneys can again be seen behind the terraced houses; the two taller ones were 365 feet high and all four were demolished on 17 June 1973, just three years after the factory had closed. No 480 will park just around the corner beyond the pub while the crew take their break before returning to Darlaston. *R. F. Mack*

Bottom Trolleybus 608 (FJW 608), a Park Royal 8-foot-wide body on a Sunbeam F4 chassis, travels along Court Road, having just passed the Gibbons Road junction as it approaches the left turn into New Hampton Road West. Court Road was laid out in about 1901, following the old field boundaries, and the semi-detached bay-windowed houses were built during the next three years. The tram service closed on 1 October 1927 and was replaced by a temporary bus route, which ran to the Courtauld's factory via the Court Road and Hordern Road loop (see Part 2), the trolleybuses replaced the motorbuses on Monday 27 January 1930. No 608 is working on the 7 service back through the town centre and on to Darlaston in about 1958. *C. Carter*

Right The never-ending repair and replacement work on the trolleybus overhead required dedicated tower wagons to enable the electrical linesmen to work on the cabling. Initially old motor buses were converted into suitable lorries, but in post-war years specially designed tower wagons were purchased, including WDA 301, a Guy 'Warrior' with a 'limousine'-style tower body built by Robinson, a Wolverhampton coachbuilder, in 1958. The linesmen are standing on the tower and repairing the overhead at the corner of Hunter Street as 511 (FJW 511), a Brush-bodied Daimler CVG6, passes the Five Ways public house at the junction of Coleman Street and Hordern Road. It is working on the 34 service to The Pilot public house at Blakeley Green, which was introduced on 16 January 1939 with a 40-minute

frequency. As well as serving the Courtauld's factory, the 34 went along Aldesley Road, which followed the valley of Smestow Brook, before reaching its terminus. *A. B. Cross*

Below Working on the 7 route, 430 (DUK 830), a Roe-rebodied Sunbeam W, is about to turn from New Hampton Road West into Hunter Street in about 1963. The area was a tightly knit community that pre-dated the massive inter-war Courtauld's factory by as much as 40 years. Most of the properties date from the 1880s through to the First World War, when housing styles barely changed save for the provision of a tiny front garden and bay sash windows. On the extreme right is a branch of A. D. Wimbush, the well-known Small Heath-based baker and confectioner. The shop was located among the Victorian terraces of Whitmore Reans, an area that had hardly been occupied prior to about 1850 as it was prone to seasonal flooding. A Wolverhampton-registered Wolseley 1500 of 1961 is parked in the shadows outside one of a number of local shops around this junction. *R. F. Mack*

Above Coming out of Wolverhampton on the 2 route to Whitmore Reans is 443 (EJW 443), a Sunbeam W4 of 1947 vintage rebodied by Roe in February 1962, while working to Darlaston is 473 (FJW 473), a Sunbeam F4 with a Park Royal H28/26R body that had entered service on 9 October 1948. They are passing the early Victorian houses in New Hampton Road East opposite the open space that led via the short Devon Road to West Park. This part of Wolverhampton was developed not as an industrial area, although ironically it became one 30 years later when Courtauld's arrived, but as a genuine residential Victorian

suburb for artisans and white-collar workers, as the houses on the left clearly show. *R. F. Mack*

Below Having passed the large Victorian terraces in New Hampton Road East, the trolleybuses climbed to the top of the hill at the junction with Waterloo Road. Behind the Lambretta scooter is the impressive Rectory with its stone mullioned windows, which, despite its appearance, is contemporary to the other houses in the area; at this time it was in use as the Corporation Housing Department's Head Office, prior to the construction of the Civic Centre on the old market site. The

Civic Centre, designed by Clifford Culpin & Partners of London and built by Taylor Woodrow of Stafford, was first occupied in August 1978 and was officially opened by the Prime Minister, James Callaghan, on 27 February 1979. Trolleybus 441 (EJW 441), a 1947 Sunbeam F4 chassis rebodied by Roe in June 1960, waits to turn into Waterloo Road as a Hillman Minx Series IIIC descends towards the distant Municipal Grammar School, with its large gable-ends. The school had opened in 1894 and, after numerous extensions, became a Secondary school in 1921. *R. F. Mack*

Above The route taken by the Whitmore Reans trolleybus service followed the former 2 tram route, turning from Darlington Street into the tree-lined Waterloo Road. The name of the road reflects the age of this Regency development, and until the early 1930s it was still a prestigious residential address. The terrace of houses in the distance even have the iron railings at first floor level that were so popular in the 1830s. Travelling along Waterloo Road away from Darlington Street on its way to Whitmore Reans is 473 (FJW 473), a Park Royal-bodied Sunbeam F4, passing Clarence Street as a Ford Squire estate car waits for it to pass. Introduced in 1956, this de-luxe model was based on the Thames 300E van, but had Ford Prefect styling; originally it had wooden trim, a feature discontinued after about a year in production, and which was also found on the Mark I Mini Countryman going towards Darlington Street. *R. F. Mack*

Below Having left Queen Square, the 2 route descended about halfway down Darlington Street until the junction with School Street and Waterloo Road. Here the 2 tram route and later the 2 and 7 trolleybus routes turned right into Waterloo Road in front of the Gas Showrooms, which had opened in 1939. Behind the bus on the right on the corner of School Street is Crawford's Sleep Shop. After the abandonment of trolleybuses from Whitmore Reans to Bilston and Darlaston on 8 August 1965, the buses were initially from the Corporation's stock, but very quickly new vehicles were introduced: 177 (GJW 177C), delivered in November 1965, is a Metro-Cammell-bodied Guy 'Arab' V with a Gardner 6LW 8.4-litre engine, and still has the factory gloss about its paintwork. *R. Marshall*

Above Climbing Darlington Street and approaching the junction with Victoria Street before reaching Queen Square is one of the rebodied vehicles that survived to the end of the trolleybus system. The chassis of 424 (DUK 824) entered service with a Park Royal 'utility' body on 30 March 1946, and re-entered service with its new Roe H32/28R body on 13 June 1959. It is working on the 7 route to Darlaston and is passing rows of mixed 19th-century shops. In the distance are the premises of the Wolverhampton Gas Company, built in 1939 with the clock on the face above

the junction of Waterloo Road, while in the distance is St Mark's Church in Chapel Ash. On the left the still fairly new concrete canopy of Beattie's department store provides shade for pedestrians and potential customers alike. *R. F. Mack*

Below left Just after a rainstorm but with the sun brightly shining, trolleybus 482 (FJW 482), a Guy BT with a Park Royal H28/26R body, leaves Lichfield Street and heels over as it enters Queen Square when working on the 2 route to Whitmore Reans. Much of the architectural delights of this part of the town centre have already been examined, but dating this photograph really well is what is coming out of Lichfield Street and passing the Museum and Art Gallery: it is a bus in full Birmingham City Transport livery, which closer examination reveals to be 1579 (GOE 579), a Daimler CVG6 with a Metro-Cammell body, working on the 4 trolleybus replacement route to Penn Fields. Twenty of these buses were hired by Wolverhampton between 23 January and 21 May 1961 during the construction of a pedestrian subway in Salop Street when several trolleybus routes were suspended. Ironically, in recent years this same subway, which indirectly led to discussions about total trolleybus abandonment, has itself been filled in. Such is progress! Between trolleybus 482 and the Queen Square branch of the Midland Bank is a parked Vauxhall Cresta EPIC with white-wall tyres, dating from about 1957 and looking like a late-1940s Chevrolet. *R. F. Mack*

Top right The 14 route to Claregate was introduced on 26 November 1925, by 6 November 1927 had become another early cross-town service to Thompson Avenue, and by 1934 had been renumbered 14A. By 1936 the aircraft manufacturer Boulton Paul was given land next to the proposed municipal airport on the Barnhurst Farm land in Pendeford. The company's 'Defiant' two-seater night fighter first appeared on 11 August 1937, powered by a Rolls-Royce Merlin XX 1,280hp in-line engine, giving it a top speed of 313mph. It looked like the contemporary Hawker 'Hurricane' Mark I, which had entered service with the RAF's 111 Squadron in December 1937, except that instead of forward-firing machine-guns it had a power-operated turret that fired in a wide arc to the rear. The concept enjoyed a period of success in the early months of the Second World War until heavy losses at the hands of the Luftwaffe relegated the survivors of the 1,065 'Defiants' to become target-tugs. That is, however, more than two years away as Wolverhampton Corporation's 303 (JW 8103), a 1936 Daimler COG5 with a Brush H28/25R body, passes through Queen Square on its way to Claregate, but diverted to the somewhat anonymous 'Aircraft Factory' during the period

between Neville Chamberlain's return from Munich in September 1938 and the outbreak of war on 3 September 1939. *R. Wilson*

Above The driver of the trolleybus waits for the police constable working on point duty to wave him on while the traffic builds up behind him in Lichfield Street, though the driver of the Austin A35 van appears to have overtaken the rear-engined Renault Dauphine (remember the TV commercial? 'A penny-farthing a mile, you ride in style – economy – the Renault Dauphine') and is now having a 'bash' at the trolleybus. Could this be a young John Hughes, one of the co-authors of this book, who today owns a beautifully preserved A35 van? The bus is waiting alongside the impressive row of late Victorian shops opposite the Museum and Art Gallery, which was built in an Italianate style with a first-floor frieze to the designs of J. A. Chatwin in 1883. It was completed two years later due to the philanthropy of Philip Horsman JP, who was later rewarded by the building of the Horsman Gardens and the well-known fountain, which was known irreverently as 'The Big Squirter'. *R. F. Mack*

Above As the Jaguar Mark 2 heels around the traffic island in Victoria Square, trolleybus 489 (FJW 489) turns from Piper's Row on the 2 route on 23 June 1963, its trolleyheads no doubt clanking beneath the overhead points. Behind the trolleybus is the impressive Sir Tatton Sykes public house on the corner of Fryer Street. Just around the corner in Lichfield Street, outside the Co-operative store, is a full-front Metro-Cammell forward-entrance Guy 'Arab' IV, working on the 34 service to Thompson Avenue. The hoarding on the right reflect the retail grocery and provisions products of the time, such as Danish Butter, Heinz Salad Cream and Persil washing powder. *D. R. Harvey collection*

Below left Standing in Lichfield Street outside the Wolverhampton Co-operative Society department store is 554 (FJW 554), a Guy 'Arab' III with a Gardner 6LW engine and a pre-selector gearbox. This batch of buses had the standard design of Park Royal body, but which was, in typical Wolverhampton fashion, not of the same standard of specification as the chassis. It is waiting for its driver, with the front wheel scotched, while working on the 30 route to the Rough Hills Estate, which turned round just short of Parkfield Road. The 30 was introduced on 1 October 1956 to serve the housing estate, which lay between the Bilston Road and 25 trolleybus routes in Ettingshall. *R. F. Mack*

Above This imposing trolleybus, 53 (UK 5953), standing in Victoria Square in 1933, is working on the original 7 route to Bilston, opened on 19 November 1928, just two days after 53 was delivered. It is a Guy BTX, a six-wheeled chassis with a Rees-Stevens 60hp motor, a type that had only been supplied elsewhere to Hastings Tramways as double-deckers. It has a substantial Dodson H33/28R body, which, despite its bulk, weighed only slightly more than 6½ tons. With a cab that looked like a small shed attached to the rest of the body, its ungainliness was offset by the advantage of an enclosed platform and staircase, though by today's low-platform body standards, the intending passenger might have needed a block and tackle just to get aboard. Careful examination reveals the bamboo trolley retrieving pole being carried along the bottom of the offside of the body. *R. Wilson*

Right A view in Victoria Square in 1951, outside Swift's meat merchants,

reveals a rare sighting of one of Wolverhampton Corporation's first wartime trolleybuses, which were destined to have short lives of only ten years. No 298 (DJW 598), working to Bilston, was the third of these first six Sunbeam W4 trolleybuses, which entered service in July 1943 with Weymann 56-seater bodies, and was only the 25th W4 chassis to be constructed. All six were stored in Cleveland Road garage for more than four years while indecision about whether to rebody them enabled them to deteriorate until the decision to scrap them became inevitable. Unusually, although they only had the single-line front destination box, they also had a side destination box, unique for Wolverhampton's wartime-bodied trolleybuses. They were also were fitted with fully upholstered leather seating. Behind 298 is an almost new Guy BT, 645 (FJW 645), with an 8-foot-wide Park Royal body, which made the Weymann-bodied Sunbeam in front look almost gaunt. *S. N. J. White*

Top On a busy day, trolleybus 612 (FJW 612) is on its way to Darlaston on the 7 route and is standing in front of Swift & Company's wholesale meat merchants in Victoria Square, just up from Railway Street. This Sunbeam F4 had the usual BTH 95hp motor and a 54-seater Park Royal body weighing 7 tons 17 cwt, and entered service on 5 March 1949; its white steering wheel indicates that it is 8 feet wide. Early in its career it was fitted with Tygan plastic seat coverings, but these got dirty quickly and the bus was quickly converted back to standard leathercloth. Overtaking the trolleybus is a Midland Red D7 working on the 885 service to Stourbridge and Kidderminster. Coming out of the distant Railway Drive is a Guy 'Arab' III 6LW with a Park Royal body, which looked quite similar to the trolleybus. Beyond the Chubb Building on the left and Chubb Street is another trolleybus on the 1 route to Tettenhall. *R. F. Mack*

Middle Having acquired some land between Railway Street and Railway Drive in 1953, it took the Corporation some seven years to overcome planning and financing difficulties before the country bus services bus station finally opened on 9 May 1960. Located in front of the Prince Albert public house and the imposing Chubb Lock factory, the bus station was eventually home to about 25 country services, mainly to the north and west of the town. Bus routes such as the 49 to Tong and Albrighton and the 36 to Wombourn used it, see here on 23 September 1960 being worked by the two Brush-bodied Daimler CVG6s standing alongside the shelters. On the 49 is 531 (FJW 531), which entered service in April 1950; the recollection is that 531 was always immaculately maintained without a dent or a scuff mark to sully its panels, and it survived until WMPTE days. *D. R. Harvey collection*

Bottom Travelling along Railway Drive in 1969, working on the 39 service to Albrighton via Tettenhall and Codsall, is exposed-radiator Guy 'Arab' III 549 (FJW 549), a Park Royal-bodied double-decker. These Gardner 6LW-engined buses had fluid flywheels and Wilson pre-selector gearboxes, which was quite an unusual option for the 'Arab' III, but which mirrored the undertaking's contemporary Daimler CVG6s; the Corporation's drivers must have been very relieved not to have the more usual constant-mesh version. The 39 service was introduced on 20 January 1947, running only as far as the Shrewsbury Arms. The bus has just left the Victoria Square bus station and has turned right into Railway Drive at a point opposite the distant curving wall; it is approximately where the present-day entrance to the railway station is situated, with the bus station off to the right. *P. Roberts*

Right Close to the end of tramcar operation in Wolverhampton one of the three tramcars from the 59-61 class stands in Victoria Square in the shadow of the London & North Western Hotel. The 7 tram route was the last Corporation service to be abandoned, on 26 August 1928. These three tramcars were purchased in 1921, having been ordered by the Corporation on 10 August 1920 and

built by English Electric as Order No 52801. They were quite modern, but because of Wolverhampton's 3ft 6in gauge these 53-seaters had to be constructed with open balconies. They had two 25hp motors and were never fitted for use on the Lorain system. The tram is waiting to load up before returning to the outer terminus of the 7 route at Bilston. *R. T. Wilson*

Below About 30 years later, standing in more or less the same place as the tram in the previous photograph, is Park Royal-rebodied Sunbeam W4 trolleybus 409 (DJW 939). It

is on the 7 service and parked with its front wheel scotched in Victoria Square, with the Victoria Hotel on the right, waiting for its crew to return from their cup of tea. Behind the trolleybus is Piper's Row, and beyond the extended canvas canopy of a tailor's, outfitter's and milliner's shop, situated between Berry Street and Queen Street, which had a typewriter repair workshop on the first floor, is the three-storey Regency-styled Clarence Hotel. This is on the far side of Queen Street, and passing it is a Ford Prefect E493A 10hp car being driven by a learner – one wonders if he or she passed the driving test. *D. R. Harvey collection*

Above If a scene shows the decline of the British car industry, then this is it! Humber was always at the top end of the market, but, under the control of the Rootes Group, a lack of investment and dated early-1950s American-inspired styling gradually reduced the marque to an unloved anachronism. Travelling towards Bilston Street and the tree-lined churchyard of St George's is a Humber Hawk Mark III, registered in Wolverhampton in March 1963. Opposite, parked underneath the National Car Parks tariff sign, is a Volkswagen Beetle 1200 de-luxe, a car admittedly aiming at a different market from Humber, but whose star was in the ascendancy with this model's total world production figure

of 7.26 million speaking volumes. Meanwhile, the approaching bus hides the cars from each other, almost dividing the rise and fall of each manufacturer by its presence. Guy 'Arab' IV 6LW 44 (4044 JW), with a Metro-Cammell FH41/31F body, passes the entrance to the ill-fated Piper's Row multi-storey car park, which collapsed in 1997 (see Part 1, page 93), before the remaining 19th-century buildings were swept away. *A. D. Broughall*

Below left Travelling along Piper's Row on the 2 route is Roe-rebodied Sunbeam W4 430 (DUK 830), heading from the distant Victoria Square on its way to Bilston and Darlaston. Following the trolleybus is a Birmingham-registered Austin Gipsy pulling a two-wheeled trailer. This quite rare four-wheel-drive off-road vehicle was Austin's response to the Land-Rover, but fatally it had a steel, rather than aluminium, body. It was introduced in 1958, and this example, dating from 1961, has just passed a public house selling the long-lost, but still missed, Atkinson's ales. Off the picture to the left is the multi-storey car park, while in the distance a Fordson E83W pulls out of Horseley Fields in front of a full-fronted Metro-Cammell-bodied Guy 'Arab' IV working on the 60 service to Bloxwich and standing in the shadow of the grand entrance portico to the High Level station. *R. F. Mack*

Above right A 1938 Sunbeam MF2 with a Park Royal H28/26R body, 266 (BDA 366) turns out of Piper's Row into Bilston Street when working on the 7 route to Bilston during the Second World War. Behind the trolleybus is the Blue Ball public house, built in 1903 and demolished in 1981 to make way eventually for the new central police headquarters. On the left are the trees that stood around the William IV period St George's Church. Despite being only 12 years old, but having a particularly flimsy version of the standard Park Royal body, this trolleybus was sold to

Southend Corporation in 1950 for just £100 and was one of nine of the class of 12 numbered 264-275 to end up running to the Kursaal and 'Sa'fend Peer'. *J. H. Taylforth collection*

Below Trolleybus 438 (EJW 438), a Sunbeam W4 rebodied with a Roe H32/28R body, has just left Cleveland Road garage and is about to turn right out of Bilston Street into Piper's Row at the tree-lined St George's Churchyard. It is being used as a learner vehicle, displaying the large letter 'L' in the nearside cab window. Unlike some other trolleybus operators, Wolverhampton trained its trolleybus drivers to pass their driving test before letting them loose on the unsuspecting public, as opposed to giving trainee drivers experience on normal service vehicles; this latter practice was allowed on trolleybuses as they came under railway rather than public service vehicle regulations. The following trolleybus is an earlier wartime Sunbeam W4, 424 (DUK 824), working on the 7 route to Whitmore Reans from Darlaston. Sandwiched between them is an Austin A35 van. On the extreme left, on the corner of Walsall Street and Bilston Street, is a three-storey Georgian property that had become the premises of M. A. Appleton, painting contractors. *R. F. Mack*

Above Operating on the 2 service to Whitmore Reans, a very smartly painted trolleybus, 446 (EJW 446), has just passed the rear entrance to Bilston Street bus garage and the large Portland stone-faced Bull's Head public house on the corner of Transport Road. Although surrounded by trolleybus wires on all sides, including those in Transport Road, as well as backing on to the main trolleybus depot and repair works in Cleveland Road, Bilston Street garage, opened on 13 May 1931, never housed trolleybuses. This Sunbeam W4 entered service on 17 December 1947 and received a new Roe H32/28R body on 19 January 1962. In this guise, it gained a certain cachet as it subsequently became the last trolleybus to Wednesfield, the tour trolley to Walsall and the last trolleybus to Dudley on 5 March 1967. *R. F. Mack*

Below Opposite Transport Road and the bus garage in Bilston Street was the Butler's Brewery-owned Red Cow public house. In about 1948, having passed the distant Victorian row of three-storey shops, 248 (AJW 48), a Sunbeam MF2 with an 80hp BTH motor and a Beadle H28/26R body, passes the pub on its way into the town centre, despite its incorrectly set destination box, from Bilston on the 7 route. A Beadle body on a trolleybuses was quite rare, but Wolverhampton operated 246-251, and 252-258, the latter being Guy BTs that looked the same, but were just over a hundredweight heavier. Entering service on 22 October 1937, poor old 248, not really that old, was withdrawn at the end of September 1949, three weeks short of its 12th birthday. It has to be remembered that Wolverhampton tended to buy bodies at a low price, so all the John Beadle bodies, generally not known for their longevity, rather like this one, were beginning to show their age rather badly. *R. Hannay*

Above right On the way into Wolverhampton from Bilston and Darlaston, the 2 trolleybus service, rather than going straight on into Cleveland Road, turned right at the traffic island into Bilston Street at the large Horse & Jockey public house, with its elegant portico around the centrally mounted front door and heavily pilastered Georgian-styled casement windows. Park Royal-bodied Sunbeam F4 476 (FJW 476), which entered service on 25 September 1948, is working to Whitmore Reans; it still has its trolleybase shrouds, which were removed in about 1958. Towering above all the local buildings alongside

the Birmingham Canal is the cooling tower of the power station in Commercial Road, supplying the electricity for the Corporation's trolleybus fleet. No 476 survived until 31 October 1964, just four days after the 25 trolleybus route was withdrawn. *W. J. Haynes*

Below Speeding along Bilston Road on a misty day is 108 (7108 UK), a Guy 'Arab' V with a Weymann H41/31F body. It is passing the yard of Don Everall; by the early 1960s Everall

had become the main Ford PSV dealer in the West Midlands, selling new Ford coaches to other operators around the area as well as buying, selling, operating and scrapping second-hand buses. Behind the Minivan on the right are the very few trees that lined Bilston Road between Commercial Road and the canal bridge. Bus 108 is about to cross the canal bridge over the Wolverhampton Level of the Birmingham Canal on its way out of town, some time after the abandonment of the trolleybuses on 8 August 1965. *A. J. Douglas*

Looking into the town centre at Monmore Green, Bilston Road is crossed by two railway bridges. The furthest, with the 'BUTLERS ALES' sign, carried the main Stour Valley railway line of 1852 between Wolverhampton High Level station (to the right) and Birmingham New Street. The nearer bridge carries a short branch line down to the wharves on the east side of the 1772 Birmingham Canal. Through the bridges on the right is Don Everall's yard, with the top deck of a second-hand double-decker bus visible. The terrace of mid-19th-century industrial cottages stands opposite the entrance to Cable Street on the left, where the road works are taking place. Pulling out sharply from the bus stop in front of the parked Morris Oxford II in 1961 is Sunbeam F4 trolleybus 480 (FJW 480) on its way to Bilston and Darlaston. *J. C. Brown*

Above The Corporation's Bilston Road tram service as far as Ettingshall Road opened on 6 February 1902, making it the first electric tram route in Wolverhampton. It took over from the old Wolverhampton Tramways Company horse tram service to Bilston, which had been abandoned in the summer of 1900, to a point about 800 yards short of the actual Wolverhampton-Bilston boundary at the forked junction at the New Inn, Ettingshall Road. The Wolverhampton boundary with Bilston UDC was along the middle of Wolverhampton Road at Stow Heath Lane, Priestfield. This became the terminus of the Corporation's Lorain Surface Contact Bilston Road tram route on 24 September 1902, after the gap in 'no man's land' was filled. Because negotiations with Bilston UDC had broken down, all the passing loops were placed on the northern side of Wolverhampton Road. The Wolverhampton District overhead tramway system had been operating from Bilston since 14 July 1902, and it would not be until 9 November 1905 that the culmination of months of negotiation bore fruit and both the Company and the Corporation dual-equipped their tramcars with both Lorain and overhead pick-up systems, finally allowing a through tramcar service between Wolverhampton and Bilston. Corporation car 20, an ER&TCW open-top 48-seater, dating from the autumn of 1902, stands opposite the Angel public house, on the corner of Ward Street, in Wolverhampton Road, about to work back across the town to Coleman Street in Whitmore Reans. Beyond Stow Heath Lane, standing on the double track, is car 19, a WDET Brush-bodied, 70-seater bogie car, which also dated from 1902, and is waiting to go to Bilston. Just visible to the right of it are the standard-gauge (4ft 8½in) rails of the old horse tram system. *O. Wildsmith*

Above Standing in front of the first post-war municipal houses built by Bilston Borough Council in about 1952 is Daimler COG5 326 (AJW 26), with a Brush H29/25R body, which had entered service in 1937. The terminus of the short 24 route to Stowlawn was at the end of Green Park Avenue in Westfield Road, having been introduced as the 23 on 5 June 1950. It ran via Prouds Lane into Bilston and on to Bradley. After the Suez Crisis at the end of 1956, the 23 route was extended as the 24 as far as the boundary between Bilston and Coseley UDC in Daisey Street at the junction with Brierley Lane. The Daimler has a body style similar to those supplied by the Loughborough bodybuilder to the Corporations of Derby and Coventry, except that the Wolverhampton examples had straight staircases. Bus 326 had the fairly unusual chassis number of 10000, making it the 1,000th C-type double-decker chassis to be allocated a number – a few were not constructed! It was eventually withdrawn after 20 years of service, being the last of the ten of the batch to survive. *R. Hannay*

Below Looking from Wellington Road towards the Mount Pleasant junction, Sunbeam W4 trolleybus 445 (EJW 445) is about to pull out round the roadworks barriers. This Roe-rebodied vehicle is opposite Prouds Lane, which was used by the 23 and 24 services to Stowlawn as well as the 75 Mondays-to-Fridays-only service from Hart Road, Wednesfield, to Bilston Central railway station, serving all the large factories along Neachells Lane. On the corner of Prouds Lane is the brick-built Central Health Clinic, opened in 1939 and surviving as an excellent example of late inter-war architectural design. Prouds Lane was named after a Major Proud, who had built a lunatic asylum there in the shadow of the Bilston windmill of 1791, which stood in Mount Pleasant. To the right of 445, which is working on the 2 route across the town centre to Whitmore Reans, is an attractively proportioned mid-19th-century house, which by this time had become the premises of the London & Manchester Assurance Company. The whole area on the present A41 road around Mount Pleasant's junction with Lichfield Street was developed not long after the end of the Napoleonic Wars, hence Wellington Road, and for many years was a 'good address' to have in Bilston. Behind the trolleybus are the mature trees surrounding the old Parsonage. In the distance, following the trolleybus, is a four-door Ford Prefect 100E and a Ford Consul II 204E, both dating from the late 1950s. *R. F. Mack*

Bottom Standing outside the Odeon Picture House in

Lichfield Street, Bilston, in 1948 is a brand-new double-decker motorbus. The cinema, designed by Hurley Robinson with a beautiful Renaissance-styled frontage, cost £30,000 to build and was opened in 1921 as Wood's Palace, replacing the picture shows in the Town Hall (see opposite) and the Grand Electric cinema. Bus 513 (FJW 513), on its way to Bradley on the 23 route, is a Daimler CVG6 with a Brush H29/25R body, and was the last of the 1948 batch of 15, delivered in October of that year. Wolverhampton had a lot of 'odd' motorbus services, which if they didn't travel along a trolleybus route before turning off into a housing estate or a factory area, like the 45 route, were inter-suburban services like this, the 23/24 route. Quite often these routes had their brief 'moment in the sun' before being replaced or augmented by a modified replacement service with a different route number. These are too many to list and frequently were never photographed, so this picture is something of a rarity. *D. R. Harvey collection*

Above right Road surfaces in the late Victorian period, even in the centre of a town the size of Bilston, were a horrendous mixture of mud and horse manure, reminding one of how conditions improved after mechanised transport replaced horses. In 1898, only 25 years after the impressive Town Hall had been built on the corner of Lichfield Street and Church Street, a Wolverhampton Tramways Company horse tram clops up the hill in Lichfield Street towards the junction with Mount Pleasant when working on the Moxley to Wolverhampton service. This standard-gauge tramcar appears to be one of the 21-24 class of six-windowed four-wheelers built by Falcon in Loughborough in 1892, and is possibly the only known photograph taken of a horse tram in Bilston. *J. Hughes collection*

Below right Bilston Town Hall was designed by Bidlake & Lovatt in 1872 in a strangely 'solid' municipal style, and was used in the Edwardian period as a cinema as seen here, with Professor Joseph Wood advertising a once-nightly performance of his silent film show, which he started in 1909. Alongside the Town Hall in Lichfield Street is Corporation tramcar 28. Since through running had been agreed in 1905, dual-equipped trams such as this operated over the Company overhead tracks. The section of the route inside the Corporation boundary on the Bilston Road service was converted from the Lorain stud contact system on 15 June 1921. Tram 28 was built in early 1904 by G. F. Milnes, and by this time Bilston had become something of a minor tramway centre. Posing in front of the Town Hall is a gentleman in a horse and trap, while walking past the tobacconist's shop is a smartly dressed woman wearing a long coat, suggesting that this view, previously published elsewhere, dates from around 1911, which was much earlier than previously thought. *J. Hughes collection*

Top In 1953, two of the first batch of 8-foot-wide trolleybuses pass each other alongside the imposing presence of Bilston Town Hall in a Lichfield Street that is full of shoppers. Both trolleybuses are working on the 2/7 service, with Sunbeam F4 461 (FJW 461) travelling towards Darlaston, having passed the old Woods Palace/Odeon Cinema, whose white stone frontage can be seen between the

trolleybus's nearside and the traction poles on the kerbside. Compared with the previous two photographs the road now is properly made up and all traces of the former tram system have long been consigned to the scrapyard – or have they, as the traction poles look as if they date from the tramcar period. Travelling towards Wolverhampton and about to overtake a parked Austin A40 is 479 (FJW 479), another

Park Royal-bodied member of the 456-481 batch of trolleybuses that entered service during 1948. This section of Lichfield Street was shared with the 25 service that came out of the distant Mount Pleasant before turning hard right in front of the Town Hall and into Church Street. *C. W. Routh*

Middle Working on the 7 route, 421 (DUK 821), a Roe-rebodied wartime Sunbeam W4, travels into Lichfield Street and passes the White Rose public house and George Darby's shoe shop. As the trolleybus takes the second half of a gentle 'S' bend it comes to face Bilston Town Hall; behind it is the Midland Bank on the corner of Hall Street, which originally led to the Market Place; today, although the famous Bilston Weekday Market takes place in roughly the same spot, it is now alongside the busy A463 Black Country Route dual-carriageway, and Hall Street just leads to the new Bilston Bus Station. Following the trolleybus is a Ford Capri 109E Coupe, the sporty-looking, fast-back, two-door version of the saloon – but which wasn't sporty! *R. F. Mack*

Bottom The Fraser Street turnback in Bilston was replaced by a new turning circle about half a mile away in Great Bridge Road, Moxley, in the autumn of 1949, because of the hazardous nature of having to reverse around an awkward corner. Once the 'Pride of the Fleet', a battered-looking 84 (JW 984), having arrived in Oxford Street, reverses into Fraser Street alongside the tree-lined Methodist churchyard in 1946. No 84 was a Guy BTX with a Dodson H33/26R body that had entered service on 1 July 1932; surprisingly it only ever received one overhaul, in December 1943. Still carrying the wartime blackout white edging paint, despite its condition, trolleybus 84 survived for another two years, being eventually withdrawn on 31 March 1948. *R. Hannay*

Above right As mentioned opposite, the shortworking 47 trolleybus service to Bilston was extended to a new turning circle off Oxford Street, at Belmont Street, Moxley, about 100 yards into Great Bridge Road, brought into use on

29 October 1949. Years before, this had been the site of the Fiery Holes, caused by underground fires in the coal seams. Trolleybus 477 (FJW 477), a Park Royal-bodied Sunbeam F4, stands in Great Bridge Road on 16 October 1963 and is about to turn into Belmont Street. In the background are the post-war premises of Woden Transformers, while facing its premises is the most modern of the cars in the picture, a Mini. Behind the trolleybus are a Ford Escort and a Wolseley 1500. *J. C. Brown*

Below One of the Roe-rebodied Sunbeam W4s, 427 (DUK 827), travels along High Street, Moxley, towards Bilston while carefully negotiating the overhead junction for the Great Bridge Road turnback. It is passing the post-war Vickers Armstrong factory, working on the 2 service to Whitmore Reans on Wednesday 16 October 1963. In the background are the last of Moxley's old Victorian houses, many of which were swept away when the Black Country New Road was first proposed. *J. C. Brown*

Top In Moxley, the site of the present-day island over the Black Country New Road is unrecognisable when compared to 40-odd years ago. In the early 1960s the trolleybus looks as if it has come from Holyhead Road, behind it on the right, which led directly to Wednesbury. In fact, the 2/7 route came from the left along Moxley Road from its Darlaston terminus. Earlier the Company electric tramcars had taken this indirect route to Wednesbury via Darlaston, and briefly on to Birmingham by the Black Country Though Cars operated by South Staffordshire Tramways (Lessee) Co Ltd from 26 May 1923 until their lease ran out on 31 March 1924. Trolleybus 614 (FJW 614), a 1949-registered Sunbeam F4 with a Park Royal body, is travelling into Bilston towards Wolverhampton and is about to overtake a DKR Dove 147cc scooter, built locally by the Willenhall Motor Radiator Company in Neachells Lane, Wolverhampton. *C. Carter*

Middle Travelling along Pinfold Street, and barely 100 yards from the Bull Stake terminus, Guy BT trolleybus 637 (FJW 637), with a Park Royal H28/26R body, is passing the Wesleyan Chapel on its way into Darlaston on the 2 route. In the background, towards Moxley, is a linear mishmash of houses of various ages as well as divers industrial premises. To the rear of 637 is a 1959 Birmingham-registered Ford Thames Trader tipper lorry speeding past a barber's shop, and behind that is a Morris Minor 1000 estate car, an Austin A55 and a Jaguar Mark I. The trolleybus is about to pull away from the marked-out bus stop loading bay. *C. Carter*

Bottom The driver sits in his cab in Pinfold Street literally powerless, having de-wired his charge within yards of leaving the Bull Stake terminus in Darlaston. Trolleybus 484 (FJW 484), a Guy BT with a Park Royal H28/26R body that entered service on 16 June 1949, is working on the 2 route in July 1961, and is totally blocking the narrow street. It is a good job that traffic levels in the 1960s out of the rush hour were considerably less than those of today. On this sunny day the driver may be looking to his left to the Butler's-owned Black Horse public house to quench his thirst. Within a few years all the shops on the right will close and gradually fall into dereliction as the properties opposite are removed to widen Pinfold Street. The road sign on the left shows that at the important Bull Stake island, one could go to any one of the 'three Ws', Willenhall, Walsall or Wednesbury. *D. F. Parker*

Opposite Tuesday 28 May 1929 was a very special day in Darlaston, when the

Wolverhampton 7A trolleybus service to the Bull Stake was inaugurated. It was an extension of the Bilston 7 route, which had opened just six months earlier. The trolleybus is displaying the number 1 on its destination box, which signifies that it is making the initial trolleybus run from Darlaston. The substantial-looking double-decker is Guy BTX 60 (UK 6360), a Dodson-bodied six-wheeler that was only two weeks old when it was chosen for this prestigious duty, though its subsequent career would prove to be short, being withdrawn at the end of October 1940. This was at a time when the nut-and-bolt-making industry in Wednesbury was still important, and small shopkeepers were continuing to prosper, such as the cycle shop on the right. *J. Hughes collection*

About 21 years after the previous photograph, almost new 8-foot-wide trolleybus 619 (FJW 619) stands in Pinfold Street with the Bull Stake in the background. The Bull Stake got its name from the days of bull-baiting with bull-terrier dogs, a brutal entertainment made illegal in 1825. At one time three lamps, powered by methane gas extracted from the sewers below, were mounted on the central standard of the Bull Stake's traffic island; the island was replaced by traffic lights in 1977 and a symbolic bull ring was placed in the newly pedestrianised King Street shopping area. Opposite the trolleybus is the Old Castle Hotel, which stood on the corner of Great Croft Street until it was swept away in the 1970s because of impending road widening. *D. R. Harvey collection*

Index of locations

An unidentified Brush-bodied Daimler CVG6 stands in School Street in about 1961, while a bus inspector looks as though he is canvassing for passengers. New motorbus services running along existing trolleybus routes were introduced to cater for people living in Fordhouses (74), Showell Circus (76) and Wednesfield (81) who wanted to get to the new Market Hall opened in School Street on 23 May 1960. These three were further examples of short-lived and therefore rarely photographed Corporation-operated motor bus services, and were rendered redundant, long after the abandonment of the trolleybus system, on 5 April 1969 as the on-going reconstruction of the town centre enabled the regular bus services to get nearer to the area on the west side of the town. *J. Hughes collection*